# Brazil

*Jan Rocha*

**Oxfam**

Available from the following agents:

USA: Stylus Publishing LLC,
  PO Box 605, Herndon, VA 20172-0605, USA
  tel: +1 (0)703 661 1581; fax: + 1(0)703 661 1547;
  email: styluspub@aol.com; website www.styluspub.com

Canada: Fernwood Books Ltd,
  PO Box 9409, Stn. 'A', Halifax, N.S. B3K 5S3, Canada
  tel: +1 (0)902 422 3302; fax: +1 (0)902 422 3179;
  e-mail: fernwood@istar.ca

India: Maya Publishers Pvt Ltd,
  113-B, Shapur Jat, New Delhi-110049, India
  tel: +91 (0)11 649 4850; fax: +91 (0)11 649 1039;
  email: surit@del2.vsnl.net.in

K Krishnamurthy,
  23 Thanikachalan Road, Madras 600017, India
  tel: +91 (0)44 434 4519; fax: +91 (0)44 434 2009;
  email: ksm@md2.vsnl.net.in

South Africa, Zimbabwe, Botswana, Lesotho, Namibia, Swaziland:
  David Philip Publishers,
  PO Box 23408, Claremont 7735, South Africa
  tel: +27 (0)21 64 4136; fax: +27(0)21 64 3358;
  email: dppsales@iafrica.com

Tanzania: Mkuki na Nyota Publishers,
  PO Box 4246, Dar es Salaam, Tanzania
  tel/fax: +255 (0)51 180479, email: mkuki@ud.co.tz

Australia: Bush Books,
  PO Box 1958, Gosford, NSW 2250, Australia
  tel: +61 (0)2 043 233 274; fax: +61 (0)2 092 122 468,
  email: bushbook@ozemail.com.au

Rest of the world: contact Oxfam Publishing,
  274 Banbury Road, Oxford OX2 7DZ, UK.
  tel. +44 (0)1865 311 311; fax +44 (0)1865 313 925;
  email publish@oxfam.org.uk;
  website www.oxfam.org.uk/publications.html

Printed by
  Information Press, Eynsham, Oxford

Published by
  Oxfam GB, 274 Banbury Road, Oxford OX2 7DZ, UK

Series designed by
  Richard Morris, Stonesfield Design.
  This title designed by Richard Morris.
  Typeset in FF Scala and Gill Sans.

Cover designed by
  Rowie Christopher

Oxfam GB is a registered charity, no. 202 918, and is a member of Oxfam International.

# Contents

# Introduction

## Bountiful Brazil

Brazil is huge in every way – in size, population, and wealth. The world's fifth largest country is the world's ninth richest economy, and home to 160 million people. Brazil's landmass occupies most of South America to the east of the Andes. It stretches from the Equator in the North to the temperate, wine-producing zone in the south. It contains most of the world's largest tropical forest, the Amazon. The Amazon basin, more than 5 million square kilometres in extent, is a giant cornucopia of bio-diversity, teeming with rare plants, animals, birds, and fish. To the east, stretching into Paraguay and Bolivia, are the vast wetlands known as the Pantanal, a birdwatchers' paradise, where cayman crocodiles sunbathe on river banks in their scores.

Besides the gigantic Amazon basin, Brazil's other regions are bathed by three large river systems, the Paraná, the Paraguai, and the São Francisco; its subterranean water tables cover an area greater than France, Spain, and Portugal combined. All this gives Brazil the largest potable water supply in the world, 20 per cent of the earth's total volume. This abundance of water provides Brazil with millions of acres of fertile land, which make it one of the world's major exporters of grain and other commodities. It ranks first for coffee exports, third for sugar and oilseeds like sunflower and soybean, fourth for cocoa and coarse grains, tenth for

◀ *A Macuxi girl, from an indigenous community in the state of Roraima, with her pet parrot*

▶ *Waterfalls on the Paraná river at Foz do Iguaçu, on the border between Brazil and Paraguay*

Andrew Couldridge

rice and cotton. Brazil is the world's third largest producer of fruit and meat. Cattle-ranching has spread from the prairies of the south to the Amazon basin and Mato Grosso in the west.

The Amazon basin is also rich in minerals, making Brazil one of the top ten exporters of gold, iron ore, and tin. Brazil ranks ninth in the world for the size of its industrial output. The local factories of European, US, and Asian motor companies turn out nearly two million vehicles a year; the aviation industry specialises in medium-sized passenger jets, which sell well to regional airlines all over the world. Brazil is a sizeable exporter of arms to the developing world. Satellites and rockets are built and put into orbit.

Brazil has the advantage of rarely suffering such dramatic natural disasters as earthquakes, erupting volcanoes, cyclones, or hurricanes that devastate so many other countries. Its major climatic problem is the periodic drought that affects millions of people in the Northeast sertão region, the most densely populated semi-arid zone in the world, where the suffering is compounded by political neglect. Other disasters, like the mudslides that bury shanty-towns, or the environmental devastation caused by forest fires, are largely man-made.

Brazil's energy needs are met from a variety of sources: most electricity is generated by huge hydro-electric dams, built on many of the major rivers. Offshore oilfields supply two-thirds of Brazil's oil needs, and a huge natural gas field in the Amazon is being brought on-stream, in addition to a gas pipeline, nearly 5000 km long, now under construction to bring gas from Bolivia for domestic and industrial needs. But the plan of the military regime to build eight nuclear-energy power stations in the 1970s failed, and there is only one in sporadic activity.

▼ *Catholic imagery is everywhere in Brazil.*

Daniel Beninson

Brazil is a racially unequal society, where discrimination is illegal, yet exists in many subtle ways. But there is no organised racial or ethnic conflict in Brazil, although indigenous communities still suffer invasion and exploitation. Although it is a predominantly Catholic country, millions of people also practise variations of *candomblé*, the religion brought across the Atlantic by African slaves; evangelical Protestant churches are growing fast too. But there is no violent religious strife either. Violence in Brazil is associated with conflicts over land in rural areas, and with drugs and crime in the big cities.

### Rich country, poor people

For five hundred years Brazil has been a wealthy country – with an impoverished population. Fifty-four million people, almost one-third of the

▲ *One city, two worlds: (left) affluent young people at play on Boa Viagem beach in Recife; (right) a scavenger at work on a rubbish dump in the same city.*

More than a quarter of the population of Brazil survives on less than US$1 a day.
(*World Development Report 1999*)

total, live in poverty, 32 million of them in absolute poverty, excluded from a share in their country's very considerable wealth. The gap between rich and poor is one of the most extreme to be found anywhere in the world. The wealthiest ten per cent of the population enjoy more of the national income than the poorest fifty per cent share between them. Officially the average annual income is more than US$4000, yet Brazil trails behind many smaller, poorer countries in its general quality of life. On the UN Human Development Index, which measures factors such as infant mortality and life expectancy, Brazil ranks only 67th. For the affluent, Brazil is a bonanza; for the poor, it is a continuing tragedy that they live in a country with so many advantages, yet reap so few of the benefits.

Over the last 500 years, the people of Brazil have lived in a colony, a monarchy, a republic, a military dictatorship, and a civilian democracy, and in all that time most of them have never been included in the process of making decisions about the direction of their country's development. The elite groups that have always governed Brazil have never seen any need to distribute income more fairly. Any serious threat to the status quo has been met with force. In 1964 a democratically elected president was overthrown by the military, because he promised social reforms. In 1989, dirty tricks were used to bar the election of a left-wing candidate who advocated sweeping social changes.

The changes needed to transform Brazil into a more egalitarian society will never come from governments who maintain the privileges of elites in exchange for their political support. Only the mobilisation of ordinary Brazilians themselves to demand a greater say in the running of their own country will bring about real change. As this book will illustrate, the process has begun among Brazil's poorest, most excluded people: the rural unemployed. In some cities, pioneer projects run by progressive local authorities are enabling people to see themselves as citizens who have the right to know how their taxes are spent, rather than as objects of charity. Education and accessible information are essential weapons in the battle for change. Through them people not only discover that there are alternatives to the present policies but they feel empowered to demand accountability and the right to participation at all levels of government.

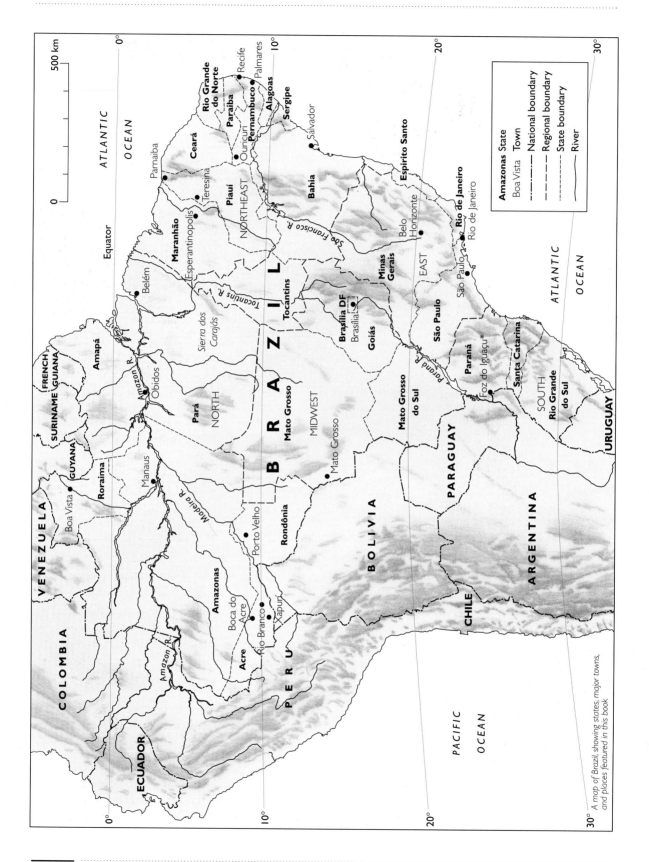

500 km

0

ATLANTIC OCEAN

Equator

PACIFIC OCEAN

COLOMBIA

VENEZUELA

SURINAME

FRENCH GUIANA

GUYANA

ECUADOR

PERU

BOLIVIA

CHILE

PARAGUAY

ARGENTINA

URUGUAY

ATLANTIC OCEAN

**B R A Z I L**

Roraima
Boa Vista

Amapá

Amazon R.
Óbidos

Manaus

Madeira R.

Amazonas

Boca do Acre

Xapuri
Rio Branco

Acre

Porto Velho

Rondônia

NORTH

Pará

Belém

Amazon R.

Sierra dos Carajás

MIDWEST

Mato Grosso

Mato Grosso

Mato Grosso do Sul

Tocantins

Tocantins R.

Maranhão

Esperantinópolis

Parnaíba

Teresina

Piauí

NORTHEAST

Ceará

Ouricuri

Recife

Palmares

Rio Grande do Norte

Paraíba

Pernambuco

Alagoas

Sergipe

Salvador

Bahia

São Francisco R.

EAST

Espírito Santo

Belo Horizonte

Minas Gerais

Brasília DF
Brasília

Goiás

São Paulo

São Paulo

Rio de Janeiro
Rio de Janeiro

Paraná

Paraná R.

Foz do Iguaçu*

Santa Catarina

SOUTH

Rio Grande do Sul

0°

10°

20°

30°

0°

10°

20°

30°

0°

10°

20°

30°

| Amazonas | State |
| Boa Vista | Town |

National boundary
Regional boundary
State boundary
River

A map of Brazil, showing states, major towns, and places featured in this book

# The original Brazilians

▶ An indigenous village in the Amazon rainforest

▼ Salvador, Bahia: A church built in the typical Portuguese colonial style

Five hundred years after the Portuguese explorer Pedro Alvares Cabral first set foot in Brazil, small groups of indigenous people still flee from contact with white people deep in the Amazon rainforest. When the Portuguese sailors sighted land on 22 April 1500 and dropped anchor off the coast of Bahia, several million indians were living in what is now Brazil. Hundreds of different nations spoke hundreds of different languages. Today that rich diversity has been reduced by centuries of slaughter, disease, and persecution to a little more than 300,000 indigenous people, who belong to 215 nations and speak 175 languages. Within a few decades of the arrival of the Portuguese, the great nations who inhabited the forested coastal regions with their plentiful game, fruit, and fish had been decimated by sickness and slavery. Some became allies of the colonisers, but many retreated west to escape from the advance of the slave traders. The Guaraní in particular took refuge in Jesuit sanctuaries known as *reducoes*, in the south of Brazil and in Paraguay. But in 1759 the Jesuits were expelled from Brazil by the Portuguese Crown, for standing in the way of the slavers and setting up 'a state within a state'.

## Legalised theft in the Amazon

Today sixty per cent of Brazil's indigenous population live in the Amazon region. Officially demarcated indigenous reserves cover just eleven per cent of Brazil's total territory. Since the 1960s, government policy of opening up the Amazon region by building roads and hydro-electric dams

Tony Gross

Tony Gross

▲ (top) Road to destruction: a highway in Rondônia, leading to a settlement project run by INCRA (the National Institute for Colonisation and Land Reform)

(bottom) Smouldering forest, cleared for agriculture in Boca do Acre

and encouraging cattle-ranching and mining has again threatened many indigenous communities with cultural destruction, disease, and death. Those who live in gold-rich areas, like the Yanomami, have seen their land invaded by thousands of wildcat miners. Other groups who lived in the path of proposed roads and dams, like the Waimiri Atroari, the Nambiquara, and the Parakaná, were forced to move. The military who took power after a coup in 1964 saw the Amazon as an 'empty' region, which needed to be populated and developed. Indigenous communities, even when they numbered thousands of people, did not count. Instead, hundreds of thousands of small farmers, expelled from their own land in the south by dam-building and large-scale mechanised soya farms, were transferred to the tropical rainforest region with the promise of cheap land. Any sort of company, including banks and airlines, could obtain generous tax-breaks if it bought land in the Amazon and cleared forest to set up giant cattle ranches. The official indian affairs agency, FUNAI, which was run by an army general, issued scores of 'negative certificates', declaring areas to be empty of indigenous people, when in fact they were home to indigenous populations.

The result was disastrous. After ranchers arrived in 1971, an epidemic of measles killed every single Nambiquara child under the age of 15. The Suruí population fell from 1200 to 251 in nine years, as small-scale farmers from the south invaded their land. By 1982 there were only 571 Waimiri Atroari left. In 1968 they had numbered 3000, before work began on the Balbina dam, a private cassiterite-mining project, and the road that slashed through their rainforest territory. Disease and malnutrition carried off 15 per cent of the Yanomami population, 1500 men, women and children, when 40,000 gold-miners invaded their lands between 1987 and 1989. Sometimes indians were deliberately murdered. In 1988 14 Tikuna were shot dead by loggers. In 1993 gold-miners killed 18 Yanomami, most of them women and children. In both cases the murderers had invaded indigenous land, and the indigenous people got in their way. Some of the gold-miners were brought to trial and sentenced, while the trial of the loggers drags on.

Many indian communities now face a new threat from legislation. A government decree introduced in 1995 allowed the limits of their reserves to be challenged by third parties, even though the demarcation process had involved lengthy studies by anthropologists and topographers. A Bill to authorise mining in indigenous areas without proper safeguards for the environment or the indigenous communities is being considered by Congress. More than 30,000 claims from Brazilian and overseas corporations have already been filed with the government's minerals-production department, waiting for the new law to be passed.

### Indigenous people unite in defence of their lands

When the onslaught on the Amazon began, indian communities had little contact with each other. In 1974 a group of chiefs, *tuxauas*, met for the first time to talk about what was happening to their communities. They each spoke a different language, but they soon discovered that their problem was the same: how to protect their land from invaders bent on exploiting it for their own profit. By the government, the ranchers, and the settlers, land was perceived in economic terms, as a source of income and profit. But for the indians it was much more. Their land contained the spirits that governed their lives, the bones of their ancestors, and their tribal memories. It was what gave them their collective identity as Suruí, Macuxi, or Xavante.

From that first meeting, demarcation – the official establishment of geographical limits which respect the area traditionally inhabited by an indigenous community – emerged as the overwhelming demand of the indians. The 1988 constitution recognised the rights of the indigenous communities to their own ethnic and cultural identity, as well as their land rights. In 1989, indigenous leaders united to form

*A conference of community leaders, convened in 1994 by COIAB, an indigenous people's organisation*

Mike Goldwater

what later became known as COIAB (the Co-ordination of Indigenous Organisations in the Brazilian Amazon), which today represents 163 ethnic groups – a total of more than 200,000 people – and campaigns for demarcation, investment in sustainable agriculture, and health and education services appropriate to the needs of indigenous communities. 'Bio-piracy' is also a major concern, with indians recognising the need to protect indigenous knowledge of herbal medicine and the properties of animal, insect, and plant life from commercial exploitation and expropriation by pharmaceutical companies.

All indigenous areas were supposed to be officially demarcated by 1993, but in spite of the mobilisation of the indigenous population, successive Brazilian governments did little or nothing to carry out demarcation until funds became available under the Pilot Programme to Conserve the Brazilian Rainforest, approved by the G-7 group of industrialised countries at the 1992 Earth Summit in Rio de Janeiro. In the same year, at a meeting held near Brasilia, 350 leaders from groups all over Brazil set up CAPOIB (Council for Indigenous Peoples and Organisations), to present their own proposals for a new indian statute then under discussion in Congress. They demanded not only the demarcation of all their lands, but bilingual schools with indigenous teachers, their own health service with indigenous health agents, and control over any mining operations on indian land. In spite of this significant mobilisation, voting on the statute has been endlessly delayed while Amazon congressmen representing mining and ranching interests propose the reduction of officially demarcated lands; one has even presented a Bill to grant an amnesty for crimes committed in indigenous areas. There are no indigenous congressmen or women, and decisions affecting Brazil's indigenous communities are still taken without their participation.

*An Ashaninka mother with her children in Acre state*

Mike Goldwater

The traditional government policy of seeking to 'contact and pacify' and then integrate the indigenous minority into the dominant culture – thus freeing their land for occupation and exploration – changed only in 1988, when the new constitution recognised their right to a separate ethnic identity. Forced integration and drastic reductions in their traditional land area led the Kaiowá, a subgroup of the Guaraní who live in Mato Grosso do Sul, to commit mass suicide. Between 1981 and 1998 there were 323 suicides, almost half of them among young people aged between 12 and 18 years. Most of the Kaiowá land has been occupied by cattle ranchers, leaving the indigenous people with an area too small to sustain them, and forcing many of them to go to work on sugar-cane plantations, cutting cane for alcohol distilleries. Treated virtually as slaves, many Kaiowá resorted to alcohol; their cultural identity disintegrated, as pentecostal Christian churches moved into the reserve. Recently they have begun to fight back, occupying cattle ranches and planting crops in defiance of judges' orders and police actions.

## Uni-Acre: working for sustainable development

In the Amazon state of Acre, however, the election in 1998 of Jorge Viana, a PT (Workers' Party) governor, has opened up a space for the participation of local communities. In Acre and the neighbouring southern region of the state of Amazonas, there are 13,000 indians in 16 different groups, speaking 12 different languages. They are represented by UNI-Acre. The leaders of UNI-Acre are actively contributing to public policies, such as the state government's plan for sustainable development of the area. They want to organise their own communities and find ways to maintain their own communal values, not in isolation, but in co-existence with the society that surrounds them.

Daniel Berinson

▲ *Evandro Goncalves da Silva, dedicated to preserving traditional Apuriná culture, uses modern technology to record interviews with old people in his village*

The UNI-Acre office is a shabby, rambling wooden house in a side street in Rio Branco, the capital of Acre. Inside it buzzes with activity, telephones, computers, and ideas. The priorities are demarcation of indigenous land and economic and cultural survival. The staff want to enable indigenous communities to become economically self-sufficient through environmentally sustainable development, not by cutting themselves off from modern technology but by making use of it without losing their own values and culture. They have a host of practical proposals: already radios have been installed in 16 villages, and people trained to operate them. They want to see at least one telephone in each area, a weekly radio programme on local issues, and respect for traditional medicine and community midwives. They recognise the need for alliances with non-indigenous organisations, people like the rubber-tappers who were once their enemies.

For years Brazil's indigenous communities were treated as passive elements of development schemes designed by governments, administered by the often corrupt officials of the government indian agency, FUNAI. (Officially indians are still treated as minors, not adult citizens.) Now FUNAI's funds have been drastically reduced, and responsibility for indigenous health care has been transferred to FUNASA, the public-health department of the Ministry of Health, which is contracting out some of the services to third parties, including non-government organisations (NGOs) and indigenous associations. Responsibility for education has been passed to the Ministry of Education. It is too early to know what this will mean for the communities, many of whom want to take responsibility for their own affairs, but lack economic independence. The Apuriná are such a community.

Francisco, Apuriná headman of Terra Firme village in the indigenous reserve of Camicua, with his daughter, son-in-law, and grandchild. 'Our area has been demarcated, but that doesn't mean everything is all right. The government can change it again.'

Daniel Berinson

Daniel Berinson

Francisco's mother Celia, a great-grandmother who still speaks the Apuriná language. She has no cash income at all. She tried three times to get a government pension, but each time the papers were sent back from Manaus because local clerical staff had written her name wrongly.

## The Apuriná

From Rio Branco, the capital of Acre state, it is a five-hour bus ride north to the town of Boca do Acre, on the banks of the river Madeira, a tributary of the Amazon. Once, this road was like a tunnel through the trees, but now we pass only one stretch of virgin rainforest. The rest has all been burnt down and cleared for herds of long-horned zebu cattle to roam behind the barbed wire fences that follow the road. At Boca we are met by Francisco, *cacique* (headman) of the Apuriná village on the other side of the river. He leads us down a steep bank to the water, where we climb into a long canoe with an outboard motor and head across the wide river. The village lies high up on the opposite bank, a line of wooden houses on stilts, interspersed with trees, facing the river. A few years ago, without consulting anyone, FUNAI installed a diesel pump to bring water from a spring half-way down the river bank, but the Apuriná have no money to buy the fuel to run it, so the women still have to climb down the steep bank to wash clothes and babies.

Francisco's mother, Celia, makes us welcome. She is small and wizened, but still amazingly active, climbing nimbly up and down the steep bank to wash her pots and pans, sometimes with a great-grandchild on one hip. She is one of the few people in the village, home to 282 people, who still speak Apuriná. Behind the village there is rainforest and a lake, an area of 48,000 hectares. Loggers and fishermen have tried to invade more than once, but the indians have managed to drive them away, says Francisco.

'Sometimes people say we must sell timber, but that would be destroying ourselves. We are the guardians of the forest. We can take trees for our own use, but not sell them. We've never sold trees, although there are a lot of people who want to. But when indians sell to the loggers, it never works out well. Even with financial problems, we've always resisted, which is good for us, and also for you.' But the community needs income. The Apuriná want to set up workshops to make and sell handcrafts, working with seeds, oils, herbs, and the other renewable resources of the forest. 'With an income we could send some of our children to secondary school', says Francisco. 'With handcrafts we could earn money. It's the only way to survive without destroying the forest.'

The villagers already make necklaces and bracelets using nuts, berries, monkey teeth, and bark. A young man in the village, Moises, has invented his own machine for making the holes in the beads. They have three beehives; if they had more, they could sell honey. They used to survive on the income from rubber and Brazil nuts, but demand has dwindled. No one wants to buy their maize and rice, either. Some of the men leave the village to work on ranches, earning at most US$4 a day. The Apuriná women have their own plans: they want to form a women's group, to get to know women's rights. They want to develop their own work with plants and herbs and make a community garden. Francisco says that FUNAI always brought them ready-made projects which ended up being useless, like the water pump, but UNI-Acre works differently. They train leaders and hold meetings; they show people how to get organised, how to be aware of what is going on. 'Our area has been demarcated, but that doesn't mean everything is all right. The government can change it again', Francisco complains. UNI-Acre also encourages the *pajés* or shamans, the spiritual leaders and healers of each village, to meet and exchange ideas.

In the middle of the village is the school, a wooden classroom painted blue. About 15 children of various ages sit at desks among broken chairs. This morning Francisco's brother, Evandro, is giving a special lesson on Apuriná culture, history, language, and myths. In a large notebook he has written down everything he can discover about Apuriná traditions from talking to the old people in the village. He describes how they used to make canoes, how they lit fires without matches, how they fished with bows and arrows, how they built without nails. He tells the children how the indians, without an understanding of money, were cheated by white men when they exchanged their rubber for other goods. He explains how the indians who have gone to live in towns or on ranches cannot live like indians any more, because they are ashamed of being indian, of talking their own language, and they are not respected. 'But the indian who lives among his own people is happy, he is free.'

*▼ Evandro, guardian of Apuriná culture, on the veranda of the village school. 'The indian who lives among his own people is happy: he is free.'*

Daniel Bennson

# Black Brazil

Brazil can justly claim to be a unique mix of races and cultures. Outside Africa, it has the largest black population in the world. Almost half (44 per cent) of Brazil's 160 million people are descended from the Africans who were shipped there as slaves. The slave trade to Brazil, which made the fortune of many Europeans, lasted 300 years, from 1550 to 1850, when Britain decided to outlaw it and enforced the ban with its navy. Brazil was one of the last countries to ban slavery at home, abolishing the practice as late as 1888. Brazil imported six times more slaves than the United States, and twice as many as the Spanish and British colonies, to work on the sugar plantations, in the gold mines, and on the coffee estates. The average life-span of a plantation slave, once set to work, was only eight years.

On arrival, family and ethnic groups were split up, to make rebellion more difficult. Children were torn from their mothers; husbands and wives were separated. Africans of different religions, languages, and customs were thrown together. They did not all work in the fields or the mines: a good number were employed in the towns as cooks, house servants, sedan-chair carriers, water carriers, labourers, and clerks. Some of the Africans were skilled craftsmen; they built and decorated the beautiful baroque

▶ *Two Brazilian boys, one a descendant of African slaves, the other descended from European immigrants*

Daniel Beninson

Daniel Bennson

▲ *Eunice Francisca da Silva with her youngest son outside their house, built on stilts over the river in Coelhos Favela, Recife. Ten of her 12 children live with her in the four-roomed house.*

churches of Brazil's gold-mining zone in the state of Minas Gerais. It was the labour of the slaves that turned Brazil into Portugal's richest colony, the principal supplier of gold and sugar to Europe for many years.

The inhuman conditions in which most slaves were kept and the deliberate cruelty of many slave-owners, who abused female slaves for sexual purposes, led to frequent rebellions and escape attempts. Those who got away formed their own free communities, which became known as *quilombos*. Most of them were soon discovered and destroyed, but in the Northeast the *quilombo* of Palmares lasted for 65 years. In its heyday, 30,000 people lived there in dozens of villages, farming, hunting, fishing, and fighting off attacks. The colony's rulers wanted to destroy Palmares, because it was a permanent incentive to other slaves to rebel and escape. In 1695 Zumbí, the *quilombo* leader, was captured and beheaded; the inhabitants of Palmares were killed or returned to slavery. In the Amazon, runaway slaves went deep into the forest to escape recapture, taking with them seeds to plant food crops.

White Brazilian liberals and emancipated slaves campaigned for the abolition of slavery on humanitarian grounds, while others were more concerned with the fact that slaves and freed slaves constituted the majority of the population. To 'whiten' the nation's genetic stock, European immigration was encouraged. Between 1888 and 1928, three and a half million Europeans arrived to work on the coffee plantations and in the new industries springing up in the cities. The slaves, no longer needed, with few exceptions were turned out with nothing, to wander the roads in search of food and shelter. In Rio they joined the freed slaves who had already built huts on the city's steep hillsides. Today these areas of unplanned, self-built houses, known as shanty-towns, or *favelas*, are home to millions of Brazilians, most of them descendants of slaves.

More than one hundred years after slavery was abolished, black Brazilians continue to be largely excluded from the wealth that their ancestors created. Surveys show that in quality of education, levels of income, and life expectancy they trail behind non-blacks. On average, black men earn less than half the pay of white men, while white women earn three times the average pay of black women. Not only are blacks more likely than whites to be arrested, but they serve longer sentences for similar crimes. Officially, however, racial discrimination has been illegal since 1951, and Brazil claims to be a racial democracy. Black Brazilians say this makes it harder to fight discrimination, because it is more subtle. In the big cities the crowds in the streets are multiracial, but the customers in the fashionable cinemas, restaurants, and shops are predominantly white. Out of 513 Congress representatives, only 11 are black. All the federal government ministers are white; the only black to be appointed was the soccer star Pelé, who led a special sports ministry for a few years. Black diplomats can be counted on one hand. TV commercials tend to show blacks in menial occupations, as maids or petrol-pump attendants. In TV news reports, unless they are sports celebrities or entertainers, blacks feature almost exclusively as victims or perpetrators of crime.

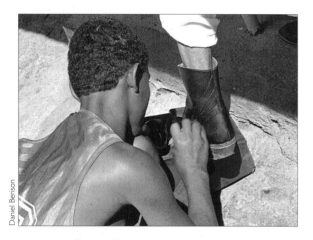 

## The legacy of Africa

▲ Shining shoes and sorting rubbish: black Brazilians find it hard to get anything other than menial jobs.

Yet Brazil's cultural identity comes from music, religious festivals, and food that were brought from Africa and adapted and developed by the black population. Brazilians of every colour regard *feijoada* as their national dish, although it began life as slave food, a stew of black beans enriched with the bits of pork discarded by the plantation owners. Bahia, whose capital, Salvador, was the country's first capital and main slave market, has contributed tasty dishes based on dendê oil, coconut milk, and seafoods, like *vatapá* and the bowls of *acarajé* sold in the streets. The rhythm of samba music dominates Brazil's most famous popular festival, the pre-Lenten Carnival. The football that won Brazil the World Cup four times was introduced by whites, but it was black players who developed the skills that delighted the whole world. Popular music is another area in which black Brazilians have achieved fame and success.

In more intellectual circles, mixed-race Brazilians have preferred to claim whiteness, like the nineteenth-century writer, Machado de Assis, still regarded as one of Brazil's greatest. Until the 1970s, Foreign Ministry diplomats claimed that the country was becoming whiter, and being black in Brazil was still a motive for shame rather than pride. Most Brazilians found it difficult to identify themselves as black or white; in answer to a census question about skin colour, they produced 134 different terms, ranging from 'cinnamon' to 'not-very-clear'. But in the 1970s black-awareness groups were formed in Bahia and São Paulo. Instead of celebrating 13 May, the day which marked the anniversary of the formal abolition of slavery in 1888, they began to celebrate 20 November, the anniversary of the death of Zumbí, the *quilombo* leader, as Black Consciousness Day. Within political parties and trade unions, small groups of black activists began setting up departments to promote their interests. Black women began to organise their own groups. One of them, Geledes, which campaigns for an end to racism, sued the Globo TV network for racial discrimination because it showed a black soap-opera character as humble, defenceless, and servile. In its defence, TV Globo argued that to portray the character in any other way would not correspond to Brazilian reality, but later another black character was introduced to talk about racial pride – an admission of the validity of Geledes' demands.

The decision to allow illiterate Brazilians to vote in 1988 gave many poor black men and women their first chance of taking part in the formal democratic process. In 1994 it probably helped to elect Benedita da Silva, Brazil's first-ever black woman senator, a Rio shanty-town dweller and former maid. But while individuals have had some success in breaking through the invisible barriers, attempts to get politicians to take racial issues seriously have not been very successful. When a committee to investigate racially motivated violence was proposed in Congress, it was shouted down by politicians who claimed that it would introduce US-style racial hatred into Brazil's 'racially tolerant' society. More recently an attempt to introduce positive discrimination and guarantee a number of places at the University of São Paulo for black students from state schools was rejected. Although it is a public, free university, most of the students who do best in the competitive entrance exam have had the advantage of going to private schools.

In rural areas, the recognition in the 1988 constitution of the permanent rights of the descendants of Brazil's *quilombo* inhabitants to land titles was seen as an important step. It seemed to give a guarantee of security to these once remote communities, now increasingly threatened by dam-building, cattle-ranching, and plantation-farming. But only 18 communities had received their titles when in October 1999 the government suddenly changed the rules of the bureaucratic process, making it much more difficult to claim ownership. Representatives from communities around Obidos in the Amazon who had travelled for ten hours by boat to receive their titles at a special ceremony were turned away empty-handed. Black organisations, fearing that the changes are the result of pressure by commercial companies interested in seizing *quilombo* territory, have launched a campaign to defend the communities' constitutional right to their lands.

▼ *One of a new generation of black women activists: Ivanete Paulina Tavares, President of the Residents' Association, Alto dos Milagres, Recife*

Mike Goldwater

# Land for the few

Although it is such a vast country, Brazil has probably the worst land-concentration figures in the world, with one per cent of the landowners owning almost half (46 per cent) of all arable land. This uneven distribution of assets dates back to the country's colonial origins. Brazil was never intended to be a society of small farmers, but a supplier of raw materials to the Portuguese Crown. So the colony was divided up into 13 huge 'captaincies' for the King of Portugal's soldiers and henchmen. The sugar and coffee that were Brazil's major exports for almost four hundred years were produced on plantations worked by slaves, not on small farms.

In 1986 Brazil's 20 biggest landowners still owned estates covering an area four times the size of the state of Rio de Janeiro, approximately 100 million acres. This extreme concentration of power and resources has led to many unsuccessful peasant uprisings over the last century. In the 1960s, armed Peasant Leagues spread in the Northeast, until the 1964 military coup broke them up. But the big impetus for today's struggle came in the 1970s, when hundreds of thousands of small farmers in the south lost their land. Millions of acres were flooded to form the reservoirs for hydro-electric dams. Millions more were turned over to soybean production on large mechanised farms. In the north, thousands of peasant farmers were driven out by cattle farming, an activity encouraged by government subsidies. For the displaced, the only options were to move to the slums on the edge of the cities or migrate to the Amazon to join one of the government's colonisation schemes, most of which collapsed for lack of technical assistance.

In 1975 Catholic bishops in the Amazon set up the CPT, the Pastoral Land Commission, to fight social injustice in the rural areas and support the struggles and organisation of the people involved in conflicts over land. The Church denounced the relentless killing of peasant leaders by the hired guns of the landowners or the local police forces, who often worked together. Between 1983 and 1997 the CPT counted 1158 murders of people linked to

▼ *A peasant farmer mourns the death of his son at the hands of a rich landowner's hired gunman.*

Daniel Berson

the fight for the land, with only two of those accused being sentenced for their crimes. The Lutheran Church, which was strong among the descendants of European immigrants, also took an active role in campaigning for land reform.

When the government realised that the movement for land reform was gathering strength, it set up INCRA (the National Institute for Colonisation and Land Reform), to confiscate and redistribute unproductive land, but with the hidden agenda of neutralising the organisation of popular movements. Landowners, rattled by the prospect of real reform, set up their own organisation to resist change, the innocuously named UDR, or Democratic Rural Union. The real aim of the UDR was to provide arms and gunmen for landowners who felt threatened, and to intimidate peasant leaders. Often violence was used to claim areas to which the landowners had no rights. *'On 3rd September 1993 about 100 gunmen evicted, looted, set fire to homes and tortured dozens of rural workers, not sparing women and children'*, reported the CPT, referring to gunmen allegedly acting on behalf of a land company owned by one of Brazil's best-known airline companies. The disputed land is in Maranhão, and the state's land agency ruled that the company had no legitimate claim to it.

▼ *'Occupy! Resist! Produce!' – a poster from the second national congress of the Landless Rural Workers' Movement (MST)*

With no land of their own, millions of Brazilians are forced to migrate every year in search of work, to the sugar-cane fields, the gold mines, and the building sites of São Paulo. Some have been duped into debt bondage on giant ranches in the Amazon, prevented from escaping by armed guards. This practice was limited but not totally eliminated after the government set up a mobile inspection team in 1995. Ranches where cases of debt bondage or slave labour are found can be confiscated for redistribution. Many of the former cane-cutters, gold-miners, or ranch-hands now make up the landless army who have joined the ranks of the Movimento Sem Terra (MST, the Landless Rural Workers' Movement), in the hope of getting a piece of land on which to grow food and raise their children.

## Movimento Sem Terra

The MST, now Brazil's most vibrant social movement, was founded in 1984 in Rio Grande do Sul, where the police and the army had been called in to expel thousands of poor peasants and rural workers who had set up camps at the roadside to demand land. Since then the MST has become a national organisation, campaigning for land reform and organising the occupation of big cattle-ranches and estates by families of rural workers. At the end of 1999, 60,000 families were living in squatter camps all over Brazil, while 145,000 families now live in 1500 agricultural settlements on what were once big estates or ranches, confiscated by INCRA between 1986 and 1996. Under the law, land considered 'unproductive' because it is unfarmed, or 'socially unproductive' because the owner has failed to meet his legal obligations to his employees, can be confiscated for land reform, but the owners have to be compensated.

The MST has successfully taken the campaign for land reform on to the streets and on to the national agenda. In 1997 a month-long march on the capital, Brasilia, culminated in a mass demonstration by thousands in the centre of the city, and President Cardoso had no alternative but to receive a delegation. In answer to the MST claim that 4.8 million families need land, the President has claimed that his government is carrying out the world's biggest land-reform programme, settling 280,000 families on new land. According to the MST, many of these families are merely having their existing, undocumented, land tenure legalised.

The MST is also critical of the government's new Banco da Terra, or Land Bank, financed by the World Bank. Instead of confiscating the unused land of big estates for landless families, the government now wants to buy land and sell it to them. This leaves families with big debts to be paid off at commercial rates of interest, when there are no minimum farm prices to guarantee their incomes. Agronomists have also criticised the programme, because in some states unsuitable land has been bought at almost twice the market price. Rural unions are excluded from the land negotiations.

**The occupation of Engenho Pasmado**

After only 15 years in existence, the MST has established branches, camps, and settlements in nearly all of Brazil's 27 states. Life in the camps, where families sometimes spend years living in cramped tents, fetching water from a nearby river, often with little to eat, is hard; but it is seen by the organisation as an invaluable learning experience.

Typical of the MST's direct-action tactics is the occupation in November 1999 of a piece of land, Engenho Pasmado, whose ownership is disputed by a sugar-cane company and the Catholic Church. Local MST leaders recruited a group of 150 families, some of the thousands left without jobs when sugar-mills in the area closed down. Collected by bus at dawn, they reached the chosen spot, next to the main road leading from Recife, and immediately began clearing the undergrowth and putting up their tents, made from the rolls of black plastic supplied by the MST. Within a few hours, the first assembly was held. Ten volunteers were chosen to look after security – the armed guards of the sugar-cane company were driving round the camp. Others volunteered to build latrines and to clean up a river to be used for washing. A communal

Antonio José da Silva with his wife Ivonne and their youngest child, outside their tent in a squatters' roadside camp in Pernambuco. 'We want to earn money by working the land ourselves. We see children begging and taking drugs in the street. We want our children to work and to earn.'

An MST protest march, demanding land and justice

kitchen was organised, because each family had been able to bring only two days' food.

On the second day, the first march was held: men, women, and children learned to chant the slogans of the MST and sing their songs. In the afternoon, separate meetings were held to organise the women and the children. A collection of individuals was being moulded into a collective group, all responsible for each other. At the meetings held every few hours during the first days, MST leaders emphasised how their strength came from acting together, not as individuals.

Once a camp is established, committees are chosen to be responsible for sanitation, health, education, security, and social life. A school is one of the first priorities, even if it is held in the open air or under a rustic roof of tree branches. Young people who are spotted as potential leaders are sent for training at special camps, where they learn agricultural techniques as well as political awareness, and if necessary basic literacy.

**Direct action and self-help projects**

In 1996, during a march in the Amazon state of Pará, police blocked the road and fired into the crowd, killing 19 and injuring 69. In 1999 in the state of Paraná, the brutality used by police to break up protests, evict families from occupations, and intimidate the families of MST leaders led to widespread protests. These were not isolated incidents. Yet the MST has been accused by landowners and members of the government of being a lawless organisation which resorts to violent tactics, because it has occupied private land and, in some regions, stopped and looted lorries carrying food. The leaders' answer is that they resort to food raids when people are going hungry. Food trucks in the Sertão region of Pernambuco were raided in 1997 because the government was refusing to distribute relief supplies of food to families in MST camps during the drought crisis. Defending its occupations of unused land, the MST points to the article in the Brazilian constitution that says that unfarmed or underused land should be made available for land reform. In addition, some of the ranches it has occupied in the Pontal do Paranapanema region of São Paulo state are located on what was once public land, taken over by the landowners' families forty or fifty years ago.

Rural unions have also fought hard for land reform, but the organisation of the MST, with its occupations, marches, and training camps, has made it far more effective. Most of the families join co-operatives, instead of trying to farm individually. The settlements usually began by producing conventional crops, but many are now adopting organic farming practices, phasing out the use of chemical pesticides and herbicides. One is producing organic seeds for sale to the public. The MST has successfully campaigned to get the Ministry of Agriculture to provide agronomists and veterinary experts. When the official credits they need for each year's farming are delayed, they occupy government banks or offices until they are paid. Most of the men and women who now run the co-operatives, meat-packing plants, poultry schemes, or pig farms were once

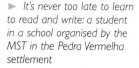

► It's never too late to learn to read and write: a student in a school organised by the MST in the Pedra Vermelha settlement

Daniel Benson

barely literate or even illiterate farm labourers or peasant farmers. In the words of Gilmar Mauro, a leader of the MST: *'One day society will thank us for transforming into citizens what the government considers human waste'.*

One of the movement's aims is to provide cheap food, produced organically, for the poorest. Besides people from rural backgrounds, the MST is increasingly incorporating other excluded sections of the population into the movement: beggars, street people, the urban homeless. For the MST, land reform is a question not merely of economic policy but of political transformation, building a more socially just society that includes people, instead of excluding them.

The government's economic policies offer no solution for Brazil's millions of unemployed. The stark choice facing many of them is between a life of crime or dependency on the 'informal economy' of casual petty trading. The chosen priority for agricultural policy is export crops produced on a large scale by agribusiness, not cultivation by small farmers or co-operatives for local consumption, although this is the only agricultural model that could employ millions of people. A recent study by the Food and Agriculture Organisation showed that families who had gained land increased their income by a factor of three or four. Towns near successful land-reform settlements find that the local economy benefits, because small farmers buy and sell locally.

Daniel Berison

▲ *Rubeneuza Leandro da Souza, MST worker in Northeast Brazil. 'I first got involved with the MST through my church youth group. Some activists came from the south and trained us in union organisation. We organised the first occupation in Bahia. Then I joined the education section in Pernambuco, and now I am the director.'*

Given the amount of farming land available but unused in Brazil, a far-reaching land-reform programme would seem to be a sensible solution to the problems of unemployment and income concentration. But the continuing influence of the landowners' lobby on government policies, plus the refusal of government technocrats to invest in what seems to them an old-fashioned non-technological solution, means that there is no political will to carry out ambitious land reform. On the contrary, funding is being squeezed as part of the austerity measures stipulated by the International Monetary Fund in exchange for loans, and thousands more small farmers are losing their land, because they cannot pay the scorching interest rates charged by banks.

Small farmers have now set up their own organisation, the MPA (Small Farmers' Movement), to fight for land reform alongside the MST, and to demand agricultural policies that will benefit small producers as well as large ones.

# Exploding cities

### Teresina, Northeast Brazil

As far as the eye can see, the dusty dry landscape is covered by rows of huts made of black plastic, stretched over branches cut from trees. Under the blazing sun, young boys wheel handcarts loaded with drums of water down dirt tracks. Women and girls sway past, balancing heavy cans of water on their heads. Men emerge from holes in the ground where they are digging wells, sweat pouring off their bodies. The sound of hammering and sawing rises into the air, mixed with the crying of babies and the music from a hundred radios. A new town is springing up, built with their own hands by 5000 families escaping from overcrowded slums. City rents are unaffordable: this is the only way out. A few weeks ago this was waste-land dotted with babassu trees: now it is Teresina's newest suburb, Vila Irmã Dulce.

### The road to the promised land

Today the school is being inaugurated. The people built this too, because the authorities say this is an illegal settlement and therefore they can provide no services for them. A construction company claims ownership of the land, although it has never used it and allegedly never paid taxes on it. A court ordered the eviction of the 5000 families, but they have successfully staged protests and appealed to a higher court. The school is a simple thatch-roofed building, open on one side, decorated with balloons, plastic flowers, coloured ribbons, and children's paintings. There are not enough desks and chairs for everyone, so most of the children sit on the floor. On the register there are 249 pupils. The eleven teachers are all volunteers, women and girls with some experience.

Adults and children are happy and excited, proud of their achievement. They sing a song about 'The road that takes us to the promised land'. Speeches are made. Leila Diniz, a tiny, spirited woman who turns out to be a public prosecutor, is the most outspoken. She talks about citizenship, about the rights they are being denied. Housing is a

▲ Water has to be brought long distances for the inhabitants of the newly occupied settlement of Vila Irmã Dulce.

Daniel Bennson

right, she says, and fighting for your rights is not an act of subversion. *'Who receives you when you go to a public building?'* she demands. *'The police'*, everyone shouts back, laughing.

The biggest applause is for the members of FAMCC (Federation of Associations of Community Councils), the organisation that has supported, advised, encouraged, and organised the families. Lucineide Barros is FAMCC's coordinator: a slight woman with large round glasses and flowing hair, her unassuming air conceals a fighting spirit and flair for organisation. This is not the first mass occupation organised in Teresina by FAMCC. The capital of Piauí, one of Brazil's poorest states, Teresina is a city with more than 160 shanty-towns and squatter settlements. Almost all the families in them came originally from the rural zone, where they were tenant farmers or sharecroppers. Some came looking for education for their children, or in need of a hospital. Many were driven out by drought, or the enclosure of their land for cattle rearing. In the entire state of Piauí there are eight million hectares of empty unfarmed land, but without land reform it remains in the hands of a few wealthy landowners.

▲ *A fighting spirit and a flair for organisation: Lucineide Barros, co-ordinator of the Federation of Associations of Community Councils, at a meeting of FAMCC's regional directors in Pernambuco*

After the singing and the speeches are over, we are invited by the new school's director, Marcia Delis Gomes de Souza, to her one-room hut for lunch. Marcia, aged 26, is one of the four trained teachers at the school. She says that few people in the occupation community can read and write, and people of all ages have enrolled in the literacy classes. *'A woman of 69 told me that before she died she wanted at least to learn to sign her name. Most of them are from the interior. They've spent their lives breaking babassu nuts and threshing rice. I think everyone deserves a chance to go to school, so we have to make an effort.'*

▶ *Volunteer teachers meet in the one-roomed home of the director of the newly built school at Vila Irmã Dulce.*

Marcia cooks beans and rice on a stove in the corner of the room, while everyone crowds on to the sofa or on the bed. There is no window, but an electric fan moves the heavy hot air around. (Some of the huts are hooked up to the mains electricity supply.) An old carpet covers the dirt floor. While we eat our beans and rice, we watch the state governor of Piauí being interviewed on a small black and white TV set. The governor, who is campaigning for re-election, is questioned about the large number of his relations who are on the official payroll. Cynically he replies that he is setting an example by keeping his family united. He also reveals that the state government spends exactly 0.27 per cent of its budget on housing.

### 'It can rain bullets here, but I'm not leaving'

Nearby, 48-year-old Maria da Graca Silva Bezerra sits outside her new home, two small rooms, with her grandchildren playing around her. Maria says she was on the city's housing list for eight years before she decided to join in the occupation. She is here with her daughter, son-in-law, and four grandchildren. Previously they shared with her mother: nine people in two rooms. Maria, an auiliary nurse, is the only one with a regular job, and the cheapest rent they could find would have consumed most of her wages. It has not been easy, carrying six or seven drums of water from the tap every day, the children getting sick, falling into holes. But Maria says she is not giving up, because this is her chance to have her own home. *'It can rain bullets here, but I'm not leaving.'*

Farther on, Severino de Abreu Sepulveda has built his family a large, four-roomed house, after spending the first couple of months under a makeshift plastic tent. He lives here with his wife, six children, and two grandchildren. One of them, eight-year-old João, lies all day under a mosquito net, crippled by cerebral palsy. His mother has taken him to the hospital many times, but all she gets there is a prescription for drugs to control his frequent convulsions, which cost the family nearly £20 a month to buy. Severino has set up a small timber-yard outside his house, where he and his sons saw planks and sell them to the other families.

Nearby, 22-year-old Valdineide is planning to set up a greengrocer's shop, buying produce at the big wholesale market outside the city every morning. Her two small children became ill with diarrhoea and intestinal infections from the dirty drinking water, so she has left them with her husband and come here to battle alone. *'Everything is a sacrifice, but it's worth it when you get there'*, she says.

The heat and lack of water have not killed the optimism of the families in Vila Irmã Dulce. They are inspired by the example of earlier

▲ *Maria da Graca Silva Bezerra and her grandchildren, outside her new home in Vila Irmã Dulce. She works as a hospital nursing auxiliary and joined the occupation two months ago, seeing it as her only chance of owning her own home.*

Daniel Berinson

Daniel Bennson

▶ *Vila Padre Cícero: 700 homeless families occupied this site in 1995, and the original mud-and-wattle huts are gradually being replaced by brick houses. The community now has roads, running water, electricity, and its own primary health service.*

▼ *Vila Irmã Dulce: build your own home!*

Daniel Bennson

occupations in Teresina, like Vila Padre Cícero, where the 700 families who occupied a piece of wasteland in 1995 now live in brick houses with running water and electricity. Most of the streets there have been paved, there is a public wash-house, and a large school has been built. Three health agents, chosen from the community, provide basic primary care.

All this was achieved by the people themselves, supported and advised by FAMCC, protesting and petitioning the municipal government. FAMCC has offices in two other towns in Piauí, besides the capital city. Its staff, most of them volunteers, work with popular movements, organising land occupations and campaigning for urban improvements. Some of FAMCC's workers have themselves been homeless or landless – like Marcelino, a former rural worker driven out by a landowner (see next page). Others are trade unionists or lawyers. FAMCC, which was founded in 1985, works to change public policies in health, education, housing, and other areas of social need. FAMCC says that the authorities make little effort to consult people about their real needs. In housing, this means that government estates are badly designed, shoddily built, and too expensive for most families. Many have been abandoned as uninhabitable, while millions of people remain homeless. Instead, people have begun to build their own homes, dig their own wells, and construct their own schools, while public money is wasted and there is a huge unmet demand for decent, affordable housing.

FAMCC plays a vital role in the planning of occupations: identifying a suitable area, making a list of families who are willing to move there,

## Marcelino's story

Marcelino Fernandes de Souza is a member of FAMCC's coordinating committee. He lives in Vila Padre Cícero with his wife Francisca, seven children, a son-in-law, and two grandchildren. He used to be a sharecropper in Soares, a small village in the interior of Piauí. He kept pigs and chickens, until the landowner fenced in all the land around the cottages to plant sugar-cane. Then Marcelino and his neighbours were banned from keeping animals or growing their own crops. The sugar-cane was for the government's Proalcool programme, which produced subsidised alcohol fuel for cars.

Eventually the landowner moved his fence right up to the sharecroppers' cottages and ordered the 87 families to leave. Most were so scared that they left with nothing to show for years of work. One old man, Francisco, who was born and grew up there, refused to leave. A tractor drove right up to his back door and threatened to knock the house down, with Francisco inside. He had to escape through the front door, throwing his belongings out of the window.

Marcelino also refused to go. He had spent all his money on improvements to his house, putting tiles on the roof, laying a cement floor to make a better home for his seven small children. He said the tractor would have to pass over his body before it demolished his house. He would not move until the landowner paid him the compensation to which he was entitled. The landowner refused, saying 'I owe you nothing'. But Marcelino knew that as a long-term resident he had acquired rights of possession, and with help from the lawyers of CEPLAC, a local NGO campaigning for social justice, he won compensation. That was in 1984. The landowner, a wealthy man, ran for the Senate in the last elections but failed to get elected.

Marcelino and his family moved to Teresina and lived in a mud and wattle hut until they joined the occupation of Vila Padre Cícero. Marcelino is unemployed now. The entire family of 12 people lives on the earnings of two of his grown-up children. One is a hairdresser, one works in a sawmill. He has a small allotment where he grows food, but this year his plants have dried up in the drought.

Daniel Berinson

organising the community once the land has been occupied. FAMCC also uses the constitution in order to influence public policy. In Parnaiba, the second city in Piauí after Teresina, FAMCC lawyers took the local authority to court to demand the building of more schools, on the basis that education is a right, guaranteed by the constitution of Brazil. FAMCC has demanded to see a copy of the City Council's budget. There is a statutory obligation to supply it, but the law is rarely invoked. The public discussion of the budget is a chance to examine the priorities of public policies.

### Two worlds in one city

Nearly 80 per cent of Brazilians live in urban centres. The metropolitan area of São Paulo has more than 17 million inhabitants, that of Rio has ten million, and that of Recife three million. Another 20 cities have over a million people each. The growth of the cities began with industrialisation

Andrew Couldridge

▲ *The highs and lows of urban life*

**São Paulo is the world's third-largest city, with more tower blocks and a denser population than New York – and longer traffic jams than any Western capital.**

in the 1950s, but in the 1970s they exploded when more than four million people were expelled from the countryside by hydro-electric schemes, the mechanisation of farms, and the spread of agro-industries, which all led to a further concentration of land ownership.

This explosion of the cities led to a sharp rise in revenue for the city administrators, but this was never matched by the provision of adequate public services for the many who settled on the peripheries and became a source of cheap labour for the building industry, or provided an endless supply of domestic maids for the middle classes. São Paulo in particular became a target for migrants, because of the booming car factories and the construction of high-rise apartment blocks and business towers that sprouted everywhere. Most migrants settled in shanty-towns on the sprawling edge of the giant city's periphery, and many spend up to four hours a day travelling to and from work on overcrowded buses.

The São Paulo underground system, begun thirty years ago, still has only 50 km of track, and grows at a rate of just 2 km a year. A few years ago a road tunnel costing one billion dollars was opened to speed up the journey to the city centre for the 30,000 residents of Morumbi, one of São Paulo's wealthiest districts. The same amount of money would have paid for 20 km of under-ground railway, carrying 450,000 passengers, or built 250 km of bus corridors. Improving the roads for the city's three million private cars has been the priority of transport policy for most recent administrations. Buses are even banned from some of the faster expressways, and bus corridors are few and far between. São Paulo's 10,800 buses, which carry up to four million passengers a day, crawl along at an average peak-time speed of 14 km/p/h. On most days, traffic jams cover more than 100 km of road.

To escape the traffic, the very rich have taken to the skies, with 300 helicopters taking off and landing from private heliports built on top of tower blocks. High-income earners in the city live in mansions or high-rise luxury apartments with individual swimming pools and barbecue areas, surrounded by trees and tennis courts. They enjoy computerised banking, and restaurants, clubs and cinemas as good as any in the world. Top Brazilian executives are second only to US executives in the size of their pay packets, and they can easily afford to hire the low-paid maids, cooks, nannies, chauffeurs, and gardeners who usually provide their only contact with the other world of the shanty-towns and slums. In these areas the

▲ *Downtown Brasília:
consumption for some,
unemployment for many*

infrastructure is not automatically supplied, as it is in affluent areas, but has to be fought for. The narrow unpaved roads make access for refuse trucks, ambulances, postal vans, and delivery services impossible.

Without parks or sports facilities or cinemas, the only leisure option for the poor is usually a bar with a billiard table. Schools are cramped and run-down, with broken windows and toilets. Researchers have found that the areas with least infrastructure in the big cities are also the areas of greatest violence. Huge sectors of the population are not only deprived of state provision like good housing, schools, and hospitals, but live in fear of their lives – from the criminal gangs who use the shanty-towns as their bases, and the arbitrary violence of the police who carry out indiscriminate raids against them. POLIS, a São Paulo research institute, concluded from a study of the city's recent administrations that the growth in violence could be directly linked to cuts in spending on poor areas that were made in order to increase spending on rich areas.

**The citizens' budget**

In other cities there have been successful initiatives to involve the population in decisions about government spending. In 1992 a programme called Prezeis was set up in Recife to enable representatives of poor communities to discuss and vote for priorities in social spending, but only in relation to one per cent of the municipal budget. Five years later, 18 social projects were under way. The idea of the 'participatory budget', or 'citizens' budget', has been carried furthest in the city of Porto Alegre, where, for more than eight years under three successive administrations of the Workers' Party, the population has been involved in setting priorities for local authority spending. The success of the programme has not only led many other administrations to emulate the idea, but has prompted right-wing politicians in the state of Rio Grande do Sul, of which Porto Alegre is the capital, to introduce a rival project called the Democratic Forum, in recognition of the popularity of the citizens' budget.

# The coup

For 21 years, between 1964 and 1985, Brazil was ruled by a repressive military regime, presided over by a series of army generals. The military overthrew the elected President João Goulart and took power with the support of the landowning classes, the conservative sector of the Catholic Church, and the bourgeoisie, who feared that Goulart would give in to the growing demands for far-reaching social reforms.

The coup was enthusiastically welcomed by the US government, which feared that left-wing politicians would nationalise North American multinational companies, and that the influence of the Cuban revolution would spread via Brazil to all of Latin America. The civilians who backed the coup expected power to be handed back to them, once order had been restored and left-wingers purged. Instead the military acquired a taste for power and hard-liners took over. In December 1968 Congress was closed for two years, the political parties were disbanded, and rigid press censorship was imposed.

Trade unions, student unions, peasant leagues, any forms of popular organisation were automatically seen as subversive. Many students and

▼ *A protest march through the streets of Recife in 1979: the banner denounces the assassination of the President of the Rural Workers' Union in Aliança.*

Andrew Couldridge

unionists joined clandestine guerrilla organisations dedicated to the overthrow of the regime. Over the years, thousands suspected of any form of opposition were arrested, taken to secret military detention centres, and brutally tortured. If they survived, they were tried in military courts under the draconian Law of National Security. Nearly 200 dissidents disappeared, while others were reported to have been shot or run over while 'escaping'. Urban guerrilla groups organised a series of spectacular kidnappings of foreign ambassadors, beginning with the US ambassador in Rio, to win freedom for scores of political prisoners in exchange for the hostages. Other groups raided banks and assassinated businessmen known to support the torture centres. One left-wing group relocated themselves in the Amazon rainforest, hoping to build an organisation from which they could liberate the country, but they were detected and a full-scale military operation was launched to flush them out. Nearly all those captured were killed, and their bodies hidden in unmarked graves.

### 'The worst violence is hunger'

To keep up appearances, in 1971 an emasculated Congress was allowed to re-open; but any deputy who dared to speak out for democracy and criticise the regime was instantly banned from political life. Elections for state governors, big-city mayors, and one third of the Senate were cancelled; pro-military puppets were appointed instead. The only space left for any sort of opposition was in the churches. It was a time when the Brazilian Catholic Church was heavily influenced by the winds of change introduced at the Second Vatican Council, and by the decision of the Latin American bishops at the 1968 Medellin Conference to make an 'option for the poor'. Christian 'base communities' were growing up in cities and countryside. These groups of laypeople met mostly in poor districts to study the scriptures, and interpreted the gospel as an inspiration for action in their daily lives, initiating self-help schemes to improve their conditions. Progressive church leaders, including some Protestants, embraced the theology of liberation, which saw fighting for social justice as the central aim of Christianity. They opened the doors of their churches to students, strikers, peasant leaders, the poor, and the persecuted. Many religious themselves paid a heavy price for their involvement: nuns, priests, and lay-workers were arrested and tortured, and some were killed. Bishops were threatened and slandered; church radio stations were closed down. Helder Câmara, the Archbishop of Recife who had become an outspoken champion of the poor, saying 'the worst violence is hunger', was branded 'the Red Bishop', and the press was banned from printing any reference to him.

Shocked by the spiral of violence and the widespread violations of human rights, the bishops, through their national organisation, the CNBB, began to denounce the regime for acts of torture, censorship, and repression; they demanded land reform and political freedom. Some, like Cardinal Arns, the Archbishop of São Paulo, insisted on being allowed to

'When I give food to the poor, people call me a saint. When I ask why the poor are hungry, they call me a communist.'
*Dom Helder Câmara*

Andrew Couldridge

▲ *Dom Helder Câmara,*
*the so-called 'Red Bishop',*
*preaching the gospel of*
*liberation during the years*
*of repression*

visit the political prisoners and tried to intervene on behalf of the
'disappeared'.

By the mid-1970s most of the guerrilla groups had been wiped out.
Under General-President Ernesto Geisel, the regime began to invest in
massive infrastructural projects such as roads, hydro-electric dams, nuclear
plants, and petrochemical plants. To finance the projects, US and
European banks queued up to provide huge loans, which in the 1980s
became the source of Brazil's gigantic foreign debt. Censorship was still
total. No criticism was allowed of the regime's economic policy, only
congratulatory articles. Even songwriters had to submit their compositions
to the censors, although one of Brazil's best-known composers, Chico
Buarque, fooled them with an apparently innocuous song called 'In spite
of you, a new day has to dawn', which became a popular protest song.

**A false dawn**

In 1975 students began demonstrating for freedom. They were harshly
repressed by the police, but Geisel set in motion what he called a 'slow,
gradual and safe' process which was to lead eventually towards
liberalisation – but on terms dictated by the military. The transition had to
be controlled from the top, neutralising demands for real change. Even in
1984, with the last General-President about to step down, when millions of
Brazilians took to the streets to demand the right to elect their own
president, the military did not hesitate to surround Congress with soldiers,
and pressure and even bribe congressmen to prevent them voting for a Bill
to allow direct elections. For the military and their civilian supporters, the

Frances Rubin

⬛ *A poster produced by artist Elifas Andreato to raise money for a workers' strike fund, 1979: 'For job security, the right to work, the right to strike, and the right to form workplace committees'.*

people were not citizens with rights but the internal enemy, a permanent threat to those in power and to the maintenance of the status quo. The transition was carried out in such a way that it allowed the oligarchies who had supported the military to stay in power, by changing parties and adopting a pro-democracy discourse. Workers who had successfully fought to regain the right to strike and form their own organisations were excluded from the new political pact. Censorship was ended, but the media, especially the powerful Globo TV network, continued to support the political establishment. Information was manipulated and selected.

The 21 years of military rule officially ended in 1985, but left behind lasting effects. The regime had put in place political reforms that ensured a permanent conservative majority in Congress and a culture of secrecy and lack of accountability for public finances. Years of censorship and intimidation left behind a tendency to self-censorship in the press. Attempts to launch independent critical papers or magazines have foundered on economic censorship: the threat to withdraw advertising. The burgeoning popular movements for social changes in the 1960s – for land reform, mass education, and primary health care – had been stifled. The emphasis was on the individual, not the collective; on consumerism, not solidarity. A generation of progressive political leaders, men and women, had been eliminated, killed, exiled, or silenced. The state-run military police forces, encouraged to act as auxiliaries to the armed forces in the war against subversion, retained their tendency to view ordinary citizens as the enemy, resisting attempts to make them more accountable to civilian authorities.

# Human rights

Brazil has been the scene of many horrifying violations of human rights in recent years. In most cases, the perpetrators – either in uniform or off-duty – were members of the *policia militar*, the police force responsible for maintaining law and order. In 1992, police stormed the main prison in São Paulo after a disturbance and shot dead 111 unarmed prisoners, many of them in their cells. In 1993, eight street children were shot dead by off-duty policemen as they slept outside the Candelária church in downtown Rio. In the same year, off-duty policemen rampaged through Vigário Geral, a Rio shanty-town, and shot dead 21 men, women, and children

Police violence has not been confined to the cities. In 1995, twelve peasants were shot or beaten to death by policemen during a pre-dawn raid to evict families who had occupied a cattle ranch in Corumbiara, in the Amazon state of Rondônia. Two policemen were also killed. In 1996 police fired on a group of *sem terra* – landless people – who had blocked a road at Eldorado do Carajás, in the Amazon state of Pará. Nineteen men were killed, and the post mortems showed that several had been tortured and beaten to death, not killed by bullets. More than 60 men and women were injured.

In all of these cases it has taken years for those accused to be brought to trial, and most of those who have been tried have been acquitted. Witnesses have been threatened, intimidated, and sometimes killed. These cases caused an outcry at the time, because they were mass

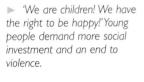

▶ *'We are children! We have the right to be happy!' Young people demand more social investment and an end to violence.*

killings, and because they were taken up by international human-rights organisations like Amnesty International. But the number of people routinely killed by the police is shockingly high. The justification is always the same: they are suspects killed in legitimate self-defence during shoot-outs. Research, however, has shown that the overwhelming majority of victims were innocent. Young black men are especially at risk, because they end up caught between the drug gangs who use shanty-towns as their hideouts and the police who raid them. Homicide is now the biggest cause of death among 15–24 year-olds in urban areas.

► *A mural in the office of a rural workers' union, depicting the violent eviction of families from disputed land*

Frances Rubin

DIGA NÃO A VIOLÊNCIA

Jenny Matthews

▲ *'Say no to violence!': a protest against the killings of street children*

Violence is also widespread in Brazil's rural zone. The Church Land Commission (CPT) estimates that up to a quarter of a million people have been involved in land disputes each year. Hired gunmen raid homes, set fire to them, ambush, and kill to expel families from disputed land. Police carry out violent evictions. In the last 20 years well over a thousand people, including rural union leaders, lawyers, priests, and activists, indians and peasants have been murdered in conflicts concerning land. In 1993, 18 Yanomami men, women, and children were slaughtered by gold-miners who had invaded their reserve.

For Paulo Sergio Pinheiro, a sociologist who has studied violence for many years, these generalised violations of human rights are the result of endemic inequality in Brazil: not just the gap between rich and poor, but also the unequal access to resources, whether economic, cultural, or political, and unequal treatment by the law. The involvement of the police in so many atrocities can partly be explained by history: when Brazil was a colony, the police were used to hunt down and punish runaway slaves; more recently, during the military regime, they were used to hunt down and torture suspected subversives and to break up protests and strikes. The population has always been the enemy, not a community to be protected. The function of the police is therefore social control, to stop people organising themselves and mobilising to demand their rights.

The other major factor that encourages police abuses is impunity.

No police chief has ever been brought to trial for the excesses of his subordinates. Until recently, members of the military police force could be tried only in special military courts, which inevitably acquitted them. A recent survey showed that what most Brazilians feel when they come into contact with the police is fear. Torture is still widely used by the *policia civil*, the force responsible for investigating crimes, to extract confessions or information. Policemen of both forces are increasingly involved in crime themselves. Out of a total force of half a million federal, civil, and military police, 15,000, or three per cent, are accused of serious crimes like murder, rape, bank robberies, drug dealing, and involvement in organised crime. At the same time, deprived of the protection of a responsible police force, Brazilians in the poorer sectors of the big cities often live in fear of death squads, vigilante gangs, and drug gangs. In São Paulo in 1999, 308 men, women, and adolescents were killed in 89 *chacinas* or mass shootings, almost always ascribed by the police to drug dealers avenging unpaid debts.

In 1995 the Cardoso government drew up a national plan for the protection of human rights and appointed a Secretary for Human Rights in an attempt to improve the situation. However, his powers are limited, because, except for the federal police, all the police forces operate at a state level under the control of state governors. The new generation of public prosecutors and judges who have taken office since the end of the military regime are also beginning to make their mark, courageously investigating police crimes, but the extremely bureaucratic organisation of Brazil's judicial and police system makes their task difficult.

Since the mid-1980s, more than 100 special police stations, entirely staffed by women officers, have been set up all over Brazil to investigate crimes of violence against women. Most have involved domestic violence, with high rates of incestuous rape being uncovered. Although many women drop formal charges against their husbands or partners for economic reasons, there is some evidence that the existence of the *delegacias de mulheres* is encouraging women to take action before threatening behaviour escalates into violence.

▼ A police station run by women for women, to deal with the high rate of violent crimes against women

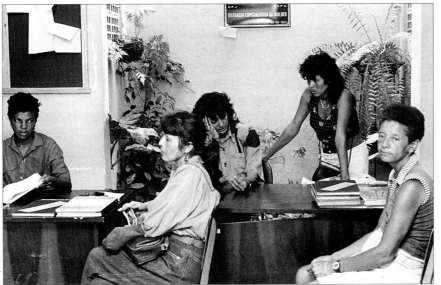

Jenny Matthews

# The political system

▲ *Brasília, the national capital, seat of government, and symbol of national pride*

Brazil's purpose-built capital, Brasília, was erected on the empty scrubland of the central plateau just 40 years ago. The central area, where the Congress, the President's Palace, the Ministries, Cathedral, and Tribunals are located, is a city of modern buildings with sweeping elegant lines and broad tree-lined avenues. But most of Brasília's population of nearly two million inhabitants live in dusty satellite towns 30 or 40 km away from the centre. Brasília was built more than 1000 km inland from São Paulo and Rio, the two major cities, to encourage the development of the mid-west and the north, at a time when communications and roads were still precarious. It also had the effect of removing the politicians from the daily pressure of the streets. Flights to and from Brasília are always crowded with lobbyists, businessmen, and politicians, but the bus journey takes 12 or 14 hours from Rio or São Paulo, and two or three days from the North. When the MST decided to march on the capital in 1997, setting out from São Paulo, Rio, and other cities, it took them a month to get there. This physical remoteness seems symbolic of a political system which was intended to defend the interests of the elite, rather than to improve the welfare of the majority.

During the military regime, election rules were changed to ensure that conservatives would remain in the majority in Congress. At that time, illiterate people were not allowed to vote. The result was that São Paulo and other states with large working-class populations were gravely under-represented, while in the rural areas of the Northeast the illiteracy of the majority of the population meant that far fewer votes were needed to get elected. This favoured the oligarchies who ran these states, and guaranteed them a disproportionately large representation in the Congress. The changes to the rules also favoured reactionary and opportunist politicians in the more sparsely populated Amazon states. They were often backed by mining and logging companies, whose interests were contrary to indigenous and environmental concerns. It was this parliamentary composition that always blocked attempts at social reforms and, in 1984, voted against a proposal to hold direct elections for the presidency.

## When is a democracy not a democracy?

Formally, Brazil is one of the world's largest democracies; it has an elected president, a senate, a chamber of deputies, 27 state governors and state assemblies, and more than 5000 mayors and municipal councils. Since 1988 illiterate people have had the right to vote, and the voting age has been reduced to 16 years. There are more than 30 political parties. But out of 513 Congress Deputies, only 11 are black, and only a handful are women. There has only ever been one indian congressman. The interests of Brazil's indigenous communities, of its black population, and of women are grossly under-represented. Among the congressmen, landowners and lawyers predominate: trade unionists and men and women from the popular movements, the landless, small farmers, and shanty-town dwellers are few and far between. This has always meant that any political advance has to be systematically negotiated with the representatives of political conservatism.

A protest camp outside the governor's residence in Recife: urban and rural workers' groups unite to demand land reform

Antonio Melcop

One traditionally powerful group is the sugar-plantation owners of the Northeast. In exchange for economic favours to keep their unproductive sugar-mills in business, while persistently ignoring workers' rights, and until recently using child labour, they have provided political support for successive governments, including the present one. In this way Brazil's dynamic social forces have been excluded from the formal political process, leaving them little alternative but direct action.

## The multi-party system

During the military regime only two political parties were allowed: the pro-military ARENA and the official opposition, MDB (Brazilian Democratic Movement). Because it was the only way in which people could register their opposition to the regime, the MDB, in spite of censorship and restrictions, grew in the big cities until it threatened the hegemony of ARENA. So in 1979 General João Figueiredo, the last of the military presidents, abolished both parties and re-introduced the multi-party system. The MDB immediately split into half a dozen parties, ranging from left to centre. One of them was the PTB (Brazilian Labour Party), which before the coup had largely represented the urban workforce. Its leader, Leonel Brizola, had just returned to Brazil after a 15-year exile, under a general amnesty of political prisoners and dissidents. But, aware of the attraction of the name PTB, and to prevent it becoming a powerful political force again in the hands of Brizola, who was a charismatic nationalist, a legal trick was used to stop him registering his new party with the old name. Instead Brizola had to invent a new name – PDT (Democratic Labour Party), and the historic PTB name was claimed by another new party, led by Yvette Vargas, a descendant of political leader Getúlio Vargas.

### The Workers' Party

The return of the multi-party system, however, allowed the formation of new parties. The most notable of these was the PT, Partido dos Trabalhadores (Workers' Party), Brazil's first mass-membership political party, founded in 1980. Union leaders who led the São Paulo industrial strikes in 1978–1980 realised that to represent workers' demands they needed their own party. The PT's first president was the man who had made his name as a charismatic leader in those strikes, union president Luis Inácio Lula da Silva, known to everyone as Lula.

The new party also attracted most of the members of the 80,000 or so Christian base communities of the Catholic Church, militants of the many grassroots organisations that had proliferated during the military regime, and most of the new rural trade unions that had begun to appear. For Brazil, the PT was a new sort of party, constructed from the bottom up, with an active membership that met throughout the year and took part in the decision-making process. This made it completely unlike the other parties, whose members were active only at election time. For millions of Brazilians excluded from the political process, the PT struck a chord: within two years it was the fourth largest party in the country, with 500,000 paid up members. Besides its democratic processes, the initial appeal of the new party was its honesty: secret deals and vote bargaining were rejected; corruption was denounced.

Branded as 'communist', politically the PT had no fixed ideological position, but only a vague commitment to socialism. It was described as a party of Marxists but not a Marxist party, a party founded by trade

Jenny Matthews

*Election graffiti in a poor neighbourhood of Belém, 1982*

unionists but not funded or controlled by any one union. Like Solidarity in Poland, the PT had close links with the Catholic Church, although in the Brazil of the 1980s this meant the progressive church which practised liberation theology, the 'option for the poor'. Yet at the same time the PT was the only party that challenged the Catholic Church's conservative morality, treating abortion as a social issue and defending gay rights. Traditional left-wing aims of material welfare were combined with the new agenda of green issues, gay rights, and women's reproductive rights.

The PT offered Brazilians a new version of politics, but it still had to operate within the old rules, designed to maintain the status quo and prevent any left-wing party from gaining power. Most PT voters lived in the urban areas, exactly those most under-represented in the Congress. Without the campaign donations from big business enjoyed by the other parties, it relied heavily on free TV and radio time to put its message across, but here again existing electoral legislation favoured those already in power, allocating time according to each party's representation in Congress.

### The new constitution ...

In 1985 the military finally relinquished power, handing it over to many of the same politicians who had supported them throughout years of repression and censorship, now gathered together in a political pact known as the Aliança Democrática, the Democratic Alliance. The main aim of the Alliance was to control the transition back to civilian government, without allowing any radical advance in popular demands. In 1988, as the result of a campaign that had begun during the military regime, Congress approved a new constitution which restored civil liberties and abolished most of the authoritarian legislation introduced by the generals. Called the 'Citizens' Constitution' by Ulisses Guimarães, the President of Congress, the new charter was later seen as a landmark in progressive legislation. But because of resistance from conservative sectors, the complementary laws needed to activate many of its articles have taken years to approve, and there are continuing attempts to revoke some of its more progressive articles.

### ... and three presidential elections

In 1989, for the first time in 30 years, Brazilians had the chance to vote in presidential elections. Disillusioned with the old politicians from both left and right, electors looked for new leadership. Lula, the PT candidate, backed by an alliance of left-wing parties, forged ahead in the polls. When the establishment realised that Lula had a real chance of winning, they abandoned their traditional candidates, and transferred their support to a glamorous, but relatively unknown populist politician from a small state, Fernando Collor de Mello. His final victory was ensured through a series of dirty tricks and outright media manipulation. Collor immediately shocked his backers by confiscating all current and savings accounts worth more than 50,000 cruzeiros for a period of 18 months, which ruined many people. He eventually resigned as Congress was voting for his impeachment on charges of corruption after only two years in office. Vice-president Itamar Franco, who belonged to the PMDB (formerly the MDB, the Brazilian Democratic Movement) and had maintained his distance from Collor and his scandals, completed the term of office.

In 1994 Lula again began by leading the polls for the presidential election at the head of a left-wing alliance, with José Bisol of the PSB (Brazilian Socialist Party) as his running mate. Once again frightened by the prospect of victory for the people's candidate, political forces of the

▶ *Pro-Lula graffiti: popular support for Luis Inácio da Silva, leader of the Workers' Party*

right and the centre joined forces, this time to support Fernando Henrique Cardoso, a former left-wing sociologist who had entered politics as a senator for the PMDB and later, with other dissidents, left to form what was at first a more coherent left-of-centre party, the PSDB (Brazilian Social Democratic Movement). Chosen as Foreign Minister and then Finance Minister by President Itamar Franco, Cardoso launched the Real Plan, a successful economic stability plan to end hyper-inflation. The timing of the Plan was calculated to ensure maximum impact on the eve of the election, and Cardoso won, thanks to the votes of the right-wing PFL (Liberal Front Party), which was particularly strong in the Northeast, where the practice of exchanging votes for favours is still strong. This gave the PFL a strong influence in the new coalition government.

In 1998 the same thing happened. Cardoso had managed to change the constitution in order to allow himself to be re-elected; but, six months before the election, once again Lula, standing for a left-wing coalition, this time with Leonel Brizola of the Democratic Labour Party as his running mate, led the polls. By this time Brazilians were disillusioned by growing unemployment, the suffering caused by the drought in the Northeast, and evidence of mounting corruption in the government. With the help of the mass media, these stories were played down, but a month before the elections the Brazilian economy was put under severe pressure as investors withdrew their capital in the wake of an international financial crisis. The extent of the problem was hidden by the government, so as not to affect Cardoso's chances. Instead voters were warned that a PT government would bring financial disaster if elected. Once again Cardoso won.

Between them the left-wing parties elected five state governors; in the federal Congress and in state assemblies, the PT, the PSB, the PPS (Progressive Socialist Party, former Communist Party), and the PC do B (Communist Party of Brazil, a pro-China faction of the former Communist Party) increased their share of the seats. Centre and right-wing parties still have an ample majority, but party politics in Brazil is dominated much more by personal and regional interests and the defence of vested interests than by ideological motives. In 1999, in answer to accusations that many Congress representatives were more interested in acquiring immunity from criminal prosecutions than in defending voters' interests, a multi-party CPI (congressional committee of inquiry) was set up to investigate the political connections of organised crime. As a result, a number of politicians at national and state level were arrested and indicted.

# The economy

The economic history of Brazil is a story of the continuing and relentless transfer of income from the poorest sectors of society to the richest. For 300 years the South American country was Portugal's richest colony; its slaves produced the gold and sugar that kept Portugal solvent. Ports were closed to external commerce until 1808, while factories, universities, and printing presses were banned. The role of the colony was to supply the mother-country with primary products, not to become a self-sufficient or independent trader.

Until the end of the eighteenth century, the Brazilian economy was probably larger and more diverse than that of the USA, but by the end of the nineteenth century it had lost its advantage. While other countries rapidly industrialised, Brazil was still a slave economy, relatively undeveloped. Unlike many smaller countries, Brazil has never been dependent on just one commodity, but – thanks to its vast territory, abundant natural resources, and privileged climate – has been able to move from gold to sugar to coffee to rubber to iron ore to soybeans. Productivity was never a priority, because it was always possible to move on to new land, clearing woods and forests without hindrance.

▲ Sugar-cane: once the basis of Brazil's prosperity. Workers are poorly paid and laid off between harvests.

▶ Iron-ore mining at Carajás, Pará, where there are 18 billion tonnes of iron ore, besides rich deposits of manganese, copper, bauxite, nickel, cassiterite, and gold.

## Industrialisation

Up until the Second World War, Brazil remained very much an agricultural country with a huge rural population. In the 1940s, Getúlio Vargas, a politician who had taken power at the head of a military rebellion in 1930 to put an end to the domination of the rural elites, began a policy of industrialisation for import substitution. He also created the paternalist, bureaucratic model of trade unionism that is still in place today and has done much to stop the development of more dynamic labour movements.

From 1950 to 1980 Brazil enjoyed a sustained period of high growth, averaging 7 per cent a year, and became one of the world's largest industrial powers. The cities swelled in size as people poured into them from the countryside, looking for jobs. With the slogan *'Fifty years' development in five'*, an elected President, Juscelino Kubitschek, took office in 1955 and set off the boom in industrialisation. He believed that the only way to reduce poverty was to turn Brazil into an industrial power, by encouraging the entry of foreign capital. He invited the big names in the motorcar industry – Ford, General Motors, Mercedes Benz, Volkswagen, Toyota – to open factories around São Paulo and build cars, buses, and lorries for the Brazilian market. In record time, Kubitschek also built the brand-new capital, Brasília, in the middle of the central plateau. The new city then became the hub of a new road network, linking previously inaccessible regions in the north and west to the more developed coastal cities. Thus began Brazil's love affair with the car and its neglect of the railways: today more than 65 per cent of all freight is transported by road.

▲ *Filling up a Fiat with alcohol-based fuel. Two million foreign cars are manufactured in Brazil each year.*

The policy of state-led industrialisation, infrastructure building, and import substitution lasted until the 1990s, when successive governments embraced globalisation and the rigours of the market economy. The years of rapid industrial development transformed Brazil: the new roads were full of shiny new cars, high-rise buildings filled the horizons of the cities, factories poured out manufactured goods. The development boom also set in motion a process of inflation and mounting foreign debt that was eventually to cripple the economy.

## The economic miracle and the debt crisis

In 1964 the military took power to stop the chance of sweeping social reforms being introduced. Workers' rights were suppressed, unions silenced, and a docile, cheap labour force became one of the attractions for

▶ In the state of Pará, an area of rainforest larger than the UK and France combined has been cleared for mining, logging, and cattle ranching.

Jenny Matthews

foreign companies, together with generous government subsidies for exports and lax profit-remittance laws. Between 1968 and 1973, Brazil's gross national product grew at an average annual rate of 10 per cent. Consumer durables for the middle and upper classes poured out of the factories; but with wages frozen, sales of clothes, shoes, and food for the lower-income groups were depressed.

The 'economic miracle' brought an influx of foreign capital. The money financed huge infrastructure projects: giant Amazon dams, highways, bridges, and energy plants. For the banks it was risk-free lending, because the Brazilian government guaranteed repayment, even in the case of loans made to private companies. But the oil shock of the mid-1970s, when prices soared, was also bad news for Brazil, which still imported much of its oil. The trade deficit grew, and the generals, unwilling to admit mismanagement, covered it with more borrowing. They refused to admit that Brazil was in trouble. A second crippling blow came when US banks raised interest rates to 21 per cent. President Ernesto Geisel still refused to renegotiate, and the debt soared from US$12 billion in 1973 to US$64 billion in 1980.

Virtually bankrupt, Brazil finally sought help from the International Monetary Fund in 1983, submitting to the IMF's usual orthodox structural adjustment plan. The austerity plans failed to achieve their targets: instead, inflation continued to rise, while the recession deepened, causing widespread unemployment and hardship. During the good years of the 'miracle', income concentration had been justified with the phrase 'the cake must grow before it can be divided'. But the failure to distribute income meant that the domestic market could not expand. Brazilian industries had got used to catering for a small but rich market, protected by government subsidies and high prices, and were inefficient and unable to compete abroad.

## The lost decade

The 1980s became known as 'the lost decade'. In 1985 the military handed back power – and a ruined economy – to the civilians. Brazilians were thrust into a roller-coaster period of alternate hyper-inflation and recession. Between 1986 and 1994 there were eight finance ministers, seven stability plans, and six different currencies; accumulated inflation in the period reached 24,000 per cent.

In 1994, with inflation running at over 80 per cent a month, the government of President Itamar Franco announced yet another stability package – the Real Plan. This plan was by far the most ingenious. It first of all 'lost' inflation by introducing a transitional currency, and then began a new phase of price and wage stability, with prices fixed at high levels and wages at low levels, which people accepted in exchange for an end to the ever-rising inflation. High inflation always hit the lower-paid worse: by the time they received their pay at the end of the month, it had lost much of its value, and they had no spare income to save and take advantage of the high index-linked interest rates. In contrast, the wealthy were able to invest and profit from these rates.

For the first time in years people had some disposable income, and there was a consumer boom. The 'feel good factor' led to an easy election victory for the Finance Minister who had introduced the Real Plan, Fernando Henrique Cardoso.

## The Real Plan

The Real Plan (named after the new currency it introduced, the real, which in Portuguese means 'royal') was a success, but it was built on mechanisms that introduced fatal long-term distortions into the economy. The new currency began life seriously overvalued in relation to the US dollar. To keep the lid on inflationary pressures, the government opened up the economy to foreign imports, even though it meant the closure of thousands of Brazilian factories and firms which could not compete with cheaper imports. Prices were kept down, but hundreds of thousands of workers lost their jobs.

From 1992 to 1998 the industrial base of Brazil was eroded: at least 1300 capital-goods companies closed down, sacking hundreds of thousands of skilled workers. The flood of cheap imports and declining prices for Brazil's export commodities, combined with an overvalued currency, transformed Brazil's annual trade surplus into a deficit. This was further fuelled by the overseas spending spree of the minority who could afford to travel abroad. For them, the overvalued real was good news, because it made foreign travel relatively cheap. Spending on tourism rose from around 100 million dollars in 1994 to US$4.5 billion by 1997.

To finance the deficit, Brazil began offering the highest rates of interest on the planet, and by the end of 1998 currency reserves had soared to a record US$73 billion. The foreign debt rose as a result, and Brazil

Frances Rubin

▲ 'United action against inflation': an unconvincing slogan on the cane-cutter's shirt became the biggest payer of profits and dividends in the developing world. By 1998 the government's domestic debt had also mushroomed, and paying the interest on it cost more than the combined spending on health and education services.

The foreign investments that poured into Brazil during this time were used to produce luxury consumer goods, especially cars, a sector which expanded at a much faster rate than industry as a whole. It was a second golden age for the car industry, which doubled production to almost 2 million cars a year. To finance car buyers, companies sought cheap loans abroad. The Cardoso government had opted for industrial development dependent on decisions taken by transnational companies – the manufacture of cars and other consumer durables – rather than developing a sovereign economic policy by investing in family agriculture, local industry, and social infrastructure. In 1997 the car industry received tax breaks from the government worth more than all the money that went to the official development agency for the Northeast, SUDENE. To maintain investor confidence, the government spent US$24 billion on bailing out private and local state banks that were in danger of collapsing.

Through these costly short-term mechanisms the government maintained economic stability for four years, and the immediate effects were good for many Brazilians. But the solutions chosen were in reality quick fixes that only postponed the need for radical measures, and continued the concentration of income. The public debt become another mechanism for transferring fabulous sums of public money to the better-off, favouring foreign investors, as well as rich Brazilians who had kept their money in overseas tax havens.

## Crisis hits Brazil

In August 1998 the repercussions of the Russian crisis frightened foreign investors, who began withdrawing their money. Brazil raised interest rates to an unprecedented 50 per cent to stop capital flight and avoid devaluation. The IMF stepped in with a loan package worth US$41.6 billion to boost investor confidence. In exchange Brazil had to introduce deep cuts in public spending. The depth of the crisis was hidden from the public, and Cardoso was re-elected for his second term, which began on 1 January 1999.

Within two weeks the crisis, concealed from the electorate in the previous months, exploded, and Brazil was forced to devalue the real by more than 40 per cent. Further cuts in government spending followed. Two billion dollars were cut from social services. The food programme for the neediest was cut by half. The school-lunch subsidy which had helped some of the poorest children was cut by 35 per cent. For some, the crisis was good news: opposition congressmen claimed that private banks made profits exceeding 10 billion dollars from insider information about devaluation. For most Brazilians it meant more hardship. Many of the 12

Mike Goldwater

▲ 'The Square of Despair' in Petrolina, where several hundred men, women, and children gather each day, waiting for a chance of casual work.

million people who, according to CEPAL, the Economic Commission for Latin America, had risen above the poverty line between 1990 and 1996 fell below it again.

## Globalisation

President Cardoso embraced globalisation as a solution for the Brazilian economy. Brazil's role is basically that of a commodity exporter. The priority of its economic policy is to guarantee the flow of payments overseas, rather than distributing income, creating jobs, or providing better social services for the majority. Without more equal income distribution, the domestic market cannot grow.

*Packing grapes for export on a fruit farm near Petrolina. Much of the fruit produced in Brazil is sold in US and European supermarkets.*

The first Cardoso government of 1994–1998 failed to tackle the economy's structural problems, like the grossly unjust tax system which taxes employment rather than profit, and basic foodstuffs rather than luxury goods. With 58 different taxes to be paid, tax evasion is extremely high. The privatisation of Brazil's state companies, many of them extremely profitable, was pushed through despite widespread protests from trade unions and popular movements, who accused the government of selling off public property at knockdown prices. The government justified the sales as a way of raising money for social investment, but it was later revealed that not only had Brazil's development bank (BNDES) given generous loans to private companies (both Brazilian and foreign) to finance their acquisitions, but also that they would be granted tax exemption for many years, effectively cancelling out the benefit of the sales. Anger against privatisation has been further fuelled by the poor performance of many of the newly privatised companies, especially in the electricity and telephone industries, often caused by their habit of sacking most of the experienced employees in order to hire cheaper substitutes.

For Gustavo Franco, President of the Central Bank during much of the Cardoso presidency, the government does not need a development policy, because its task is to clear the way for the action of money and markets. For President Cardoso, speaking at a meeting in 1996, social exclusion and social regression are inevitable consequences of globalisation. For Brazil's popular movements, poverty and social exclusion are not inevitable, and public policies need to be changed so that they distribute income, instead of concentrating it.

# Communications

### The power of television

The extremely high illiteracy rate, with two out of every five people either illiterate or functionally illiterate, has not prevented Brazil from developing a highly sophisticated media industry. But it has meant leaping straight from the oral culture of a slave society to the audio-visual culture of a post-modern society where television and radio, not the written word, provide most people with news and information.

► Even the poorest homes have TV sets: Edileusa Severina do Santana and her grand-daughter Paulina at home in a favela in Recife.

Daniel Berinson

TV ownership soared under the repressive 21-year military regime, because the generals realised that it could be a useful tool of social control. Easy hire-purchase terms meant that even the poorest could buy a set, and aerials soon sprouted over even the most dilapidated shack. Television news was carefully pruned of anything unwelcome to the military; long, detailed telexes with lists of subjects to be omitted or downplayed were sent daily to the TV stations. Hours of romantic 'soaps' and variety shows were screened, offering ordinary people an escape from the struggle of their daily lives.

Under civilian government, direct censorship no longer exists, but television channels, owned by commercial groups that depend on government advertising revenues and patronage, tend to defend the status

▲ *Film posters promise an escape from the problems of daily life.*

quo. Seven families control the media groups that own most of Brazil's TV and radio stations, and newspapers. The Globo Network, owned by the Marinho family, predominates over all the others, with an audience share of 50–60 per cent. With more than 100 regional TV stations, 50 radio stations, and a cable TV channel, it is the fourth-largest television network in the world, exporting soaps to Africa, China, Latin America, and Europe. Although its soaps now tackle questions like sexual preferences, AIDS, and surrogate motherhood, they still avoid questions of race and class. Technically and commercially, Globo is a huge success story. But Globo is much more than a purveyor of entertainment, news, and occasional documentaries. It is also an active player in the political arena, manipulating the news agenda to suit the interests of the government in power, or the electoral candidates whom it supports. In the 1989 presidential elections, when the candidate of the popular movements, the Workers' Party's Luis Inácio Lula da Silva, stood a real chance of winning, TV Globo showed footage unfavourable to him, including false accusations, and manipulated the images of the candidates during the final TV debate. In this it was not alone, because business, finance, and landowning interests had decided that Lula had to be defeated at all costs, and all the major newspapers and TV and radio stations transmitted myths and distortions about the left-wing candidate; but Globo's power and influence were much greater than the others.

The Brazilian media played the same role in the 1994 campaign, when Lula ran against Fernando Henrique Cardoso: 85 per cent of column inches were devoted to Cardoso, and only 15 per cent to Lula. When, in spite of this, Lula forged ahead in the opinion polls, he and the PT were falsely accused of involvement in various crimes. Cardoso won. In 1998, when Lula once more challenged Fernando Henrique Cardoso for the presidency and led the polls, the President called a meeting of media barons and asked them to stop giving space to 'negative' news, like the drought and unemployment. Instead they were encouraged to launch the Feel Good Campaign, using yellow, blue, and green, the colours of the Brazilian flag and Cardoso's election propaganda. In October a major financial crisis hit Brazil on the eve of the election. Globo's main evening news bulletin devoted just one minute to it, and nine minutes to the birth of the baby of one of the TV network's favourite performers, Xuxa. Although the crisis had been brought about partly by the Cardoso government's own policies, the media almost exclusively blamed foreign speculators and poured scorn on the PT's ability to deal with such a crisis. Cardoso won again.

## Licences to print money

The origin of this political use of the media goes back to the undemocratic way in which licences to run television and radio stations are distributed. Successive governments have handed them out as favours to congressmen or their protégés in return for political support. The last of the general-presidents, João Figueiredo, distributed 634 TV and radio frequencies during his six years in office, many of them to congressmen in exchange for voting against the Bill restoring direct elections. Between 1985 and 1989 President José Sarney handed out more than 1000 franchises, 539 of them to congressmen or their relations in exchange for voting for a Bill to extend his mandate a further year. Sarney himself controls 35 of the 57 radio and TV stations in his home state, Maranhão. The practice has continued since then.

Nobody who has won a concession like this has ever had to submit a programming proposal. Rather the franchises have been seen as licences to print money and elect certain candidates. Evangelical churches whose leaders support conservative politicians have also won radio and TV frequencies; but requests from popular movements, trade unions, or progressive churches to run educational stations have invariably been refused.

Compared with the influence of television and radio on the general population, newspapers reach very few people. Together, the four major dailies sell 1.5 million copies for a population of 160 million. The total daily circulation of Brazil's 400 dailies adds up to only 6.9 million copies. With a readership largely confined to the middle and upper classes, the result is that newspapers reflect the lives and opinions of their readers, rather than those of the vast majority of the population.

The biggest opportunity for democratic communication lies with radio. Over 90 per cent of Brazilian homes have a radio. Local community radio stations have begun to spring up, run on shoestring budgets by popular movements and non-government organisations (NGOs). Their frequency is legally limited to a few kilometres, but, especially in the 3000 municipalities that have no other radio station, they offer a space for the dissemination of democratic information on local issues and the broadcast of educational programmes, to counterbalance the political propaganda and misinformation conveyed by so many of the bigger stations.

One NGO that is making good use of local radio is the Catholic Church's Children's Pastoral. It has pioneered a low-cost system of making and distributing tapes containing information on child-care and nutrition to more than 1000 local radio stations, both religious and commercial.

# Education

Thirteen-year-old Luciana stands on the broken wooden boards outside her shanty-town home in Rio. Below her, a fetid stream carries sewage into the Bay of Guanabara. She says she wants to be a computer programmer and points with pride to her school, a large concrete building with oval windows which rises beyond the shanty-town. It is one of scores of new purpose-built schools constructed between 1982 and 1986 by Rio's then governor Leonel Brizola, of the PDT (Democratic Labour Party), in an ambitious programme to provide a first-class education for Rio's most underprivileged children. Designed by Brazil's most famous architect, Oscar Niemeyer, they were located in some of the worst slum areas and provided not only lessons, but a library, sports facilities, showers, and three meals a day – things not normally available in state schools. For a few years the distinctive shape of a Centre for Integrated Popular Education (CIEP), the schools' official name, rising above the crowded shacks of a shanty-town, represented hope, the chance of escape through education. But the CIEPs were expensive to run, and Brizola's successor and political enemy did not give them the same priority in his budget, so that their quality declined to the level of other schools.

Most state schools still offer children a poor education. Ninety-four out of every 100 poor children are enrolled at 7 years old for primary school. At the end of four years, only 50 are still in the classroom, and only 15 of them complete nine years of schooling. Repetition is one of the main causes: pupils who fail to do well in end-of-year examinations are forced to repeat the entire year, sometimes two, three, or even four times. This means that classes contain pupils of many different ages. Brazilians spend less than five years at school on average, compared with almost nine years in Chile and Argentina.

Yet Brazil's per capita spending on education is as high as countries where literacy rates are much better. The problem is the way in which the money is distributed. Sixty per cent of the federal education budget is spent on state universities, where average student/lecturer ratios are much

*'State schooling is everyone's right': a demonstration demanding more government investment in education*

lower than in many industrialised countries (6.5 students per lecturer, compared with 23 in France). Ironically the majority of the students at the public, free universities come from middle-income or rich families and have had the advantage of a private-school education. Primary education is the responsibility of local authorities, and, in the poorer states, unqualified, underpaid teachers work in over-crowded, under-resourced schools, with few books or equipment, many of them without running water or toilets.

## No uniform, no education

Mike Goldwater

Although primary education is free, poor families have to overcome many obstacles. Until recently registry offices, which are privately owned, charged up to £10 for a birth certificate, without which a child cannot be enrolled. In 1999 a Bill was passed to make them free, although many registry offices, reluctant to lose a profitable source of income, still create difficulties for poor families. At the beginning of each term, parents are given a long list of materials they must supply; it includes not only books, pencils, crayons, and paper for their own child, but office supplies for the school administration. Without a uniform, which the family must also pay for, the child risks being sent home. Nearly all schools operate on a shift system, with three or four shifts using the same classrooms every day. Secondary schools have an evening shift for adolescents who work during the day. This means that the average school day is only three to four hours long. Another problem is the high drop-out rate. For many poor families, the main incentive to send their child to school is the school meals. Since 1994, the government has introduced a series of measures to try to improve primary schooling. All teachers' pay is supposed to be topped up to at least R$300 (US$180) a month by a federal fund. School textbooks will be designed to last for several years, instead of being discarded at the end of each year, which was a very profitable system for the publishers.

## No education, no democracy

Brazilian elites have never seen the need for a good education system, because an ignorant illiterate population has been easier to manipulate and control. The result is one of the highest illiteracy rates in Latin America. Nineteen per cent of adult Brazilians, almost one fifth, cannot read or write, and probably the same proportion are 'functionally illiterate': they know only how to write their names. An Inter-American Development Bank report on inequality in Latin America for 1998–1999 found that because education is so profoundly stratified in the region it is perpetuating disparities in incomes, rather than correcting them, and that Brazil, which had the worst gap between rich and poor, was one of the worst offenders. The report found that in Brazil, unlike elsewhere, education is not a mechanism for social mobility or reducing income differences, because the quality of education offered to students from high-income and low-income families is so different. For the Bank, the problem is not the level of expenditure, but the organisation of the public education system, which fails to provide incentives to improve quality and to involve families or even teachers in decisions about education. The Bank suggested that families should be given direct subsidies for books, transport, uniforms, and meals.

## A different kind of education

The Landless Rural Workers' Movement (MST) has made education a priority in its camps and settlements from the beginning. In the camps, where families live in black plastic tents for months or even years, waiting for land, the school takes pride of place, even if it is a rustic building made, like the tents, of black plastic stretched over branches, and the pupils have to sit on tree trunks. On the more established settlements in Rio Grande do Sul, the school is surrounded by sports fields, vegetable gardens that are tended by the pupils, and flower beds. The MST runs its own teacher-training courses, so that, besides teaching basic literacy and numeracy, they can encourage the children to acquire a more critical vision of what goes on in Brazil, and grow up to put collective values above consumerism and individualism.

Observers have noted that children who have attended MST schools are more questioning and less passive than others. In one MST school, the teachers set up a camp-like black plastic tent on the lawn, so the children could see what their parents had endured to acquire their land. Many indigenous communities are now setting up bilingual schools where their own culture is part of the curriculum, as they are entitled to do under the Constitution. Among them are the Mura and the Xucuru, who have produced a book of their own stories. In 1995 the CCPY (the Pro-Yanomami Commission) began an education project with the Yanomami in the village of Demeni. The pupils, of all ages and both sexes, are taught to read and write, first in their own language and then in Portuguese.

Daniel Berinson

▲ *A makeshift school in the squatters' settlement of Pedra Vermelha*

▼ *Jeronimo de Oliveira, a teacher at a COIAB school for Macuxi children. 'Here our children learn to read and write in their maternal language. My mother didn't talk to me in Macuxi, because the whites had taught her to be ashamed of it.'*

Young Yanomami responded to the project with huge enthusiasm, and handwritten letters are now exchanged between villages. In their drawings the children illustrate their myths and beliefs. Those who do especially well in the local schools go on for further language-training in Boa Vista, and can become either teachers or clinic assistants within the health programme. Learning Portuguese and mathematics is an essential preparation for the economic projects that the Yanomami want to develop.

Mike Goldwater

# Children at work

C. de Godoy

▼ For one day's exhausting labour on a sugar-cane plantation, this boy, whose family cannot afford to keep him in school, will earn about one dollar.

On a steep hillside in the hot sun, 12-year-old Juliano cuts cane alongside his father. He began the day at 3am with a cup of black coffee, before setting out on the long walk to reach the sugar-cane field by 6am. His feet, protected only by a pair of worn rubber-thong sandals, are covered in cuts from the sharp-edged cane. His face is smudged and his hands blackened by the cane. For a day's backbreaking work he will earn about US$1.00, but it is a vital contribution towards his family's income. At home he has five younger brothers and sisters.

In 1996 there were 60,000 children like Juliano cutting cane in the Northeast. A survey carried out by the Josué de Castro research centre, an NGO in Recife, found that half of them had been injured because they were using tools designed for adults. *'When I was seven, I trod on a scythe. I had to have 20 stitches. My mum took me to hospital'*, recalls Maria José, *now 12 years old. 'It makes you sleepy. You get tired, you fall asleep doing your homework. You get home at 10, then you've got to wake up at half past three in the morning'*, says Flavio, aged eleven, who attends school after work.

## Where childhood ends at 5

In many parts of the Amazon basin, boys and girls as young as 5 or 6 work alongside their parents, stoking and unloading the mud kilns used for burning wood to produce charcoal. Their feet get burnt from the hot coals. Each family has to tend 10 to 20 kilns, day and night, living in makeshift camps, often deep in the forest. In Mato Grosso do Sul until recently, more than 6000 children were at work in the ovens, while small children played and slept in the filthy smoky air of the kilns, because their mothers had nowhere else to leave them. Many of the families are hired in shanty-towns and driven to the camps, where they find themselves trapped into debt, owing money to their employers for tools, food, and transport. As most of the adults are illiterate, they cannot check or control what is deducted from their pay, and they are usually cheated.

On the rubbish dump: a young scavenger in Recife

In other places children work all day long, breaking stones or feeding sisal into machines to make rope, or making bricks. In the cities, children can be seen selling sweets, flowers, or fruit outside restaurants, or at traffic lights. According to UNICEF, another 50,000 children and adolescents work in city rubbish dumps, looking for edible food or tins or bottles to be recycled; or spend the night hours helping their parents to collect and select the waste left on the pavements by shops and offices. These children pull carts and carry heavy loads to earn US$ 1.50 a day if they are lucky. On the dumps they are at risk of being cut by bits of glass, rusty pieces of iron, and hospital needles, catching skin diseases or becoming ill from eating contaminated food. In many Brazilian homes, girls of 13 or 14, sometimes younger, work long hours as domestic maids or nursemaids, at the beck and call of an entire family, sleeping in cramped rooms, to earn a pittance. In the Amazon, young teenage girls can be found in roadside bars and brothels, working as prostitutes; cities like Manaus and Porto Velho have hundreds of child prostitutes.

Altogether an estimated three and a half million children work in Brazil. Ninety per cent of them began work between the ages of 7 and 13. In the 1990s, growing awareness of the problem led the government to announce plans to eradicate it altogether. It was recognised that for poor families the children's contribution, however small, was essential, and therefore families had to be compensated. The first such programme, launched in 1995 by the Governor of Brasília, Cristovam Buarque, of the Workers' Party, paid families half a minimum salary for each child who went to school on a regular basis. This scheme was then adopted by the federal government and extended to several thousand children in the charcoal and sugar-cane industries and in cassiterite mines in the Amazon. In some places schools were specially built near the sugar-cane fields or charcoal kilns. Besides lessons, the children get school meals.

In 1999 the programme suffered setbacks. In Brasília Governor Buarque failed to get re-elected, and his successor, a right-wing populist, replaced the scheme with handouts of books and uniforms. At a federal level the programme has been undermined by public spending cuts to meet the financial targets determined by the International Monetary Fund. Left without the government allowance for months at a time, many families were forced to send their children back to work. In 1999 UNICEF and Brazilian NGOs launched a campaign to get several thousand children out of the rubbish dumps where they sort waste, by the year 2002. In one city, Belo Horizonte, street waste is now taken to be sorted at shelters where child-care facilities are provided.

In the cities many children who work on the streets end up living on the streets, or going home infrequently. For some, the freedom of street life is preferable to a life of hunger, overcrowding, and abuse at home. But on the streets children are a regular target for death squads, vigilante gangs, drug dealers, and brutal policemen. To dull hunger they sniff glue: to buy it, they beg, shoplift, and prostitute themselves.

# Health

One of the first things that a visitor to Brazil notices is the large number of well-stocked pharmacies everywhere. Self-medication is widespread, and the pharmacies not only dispense prescription medicines without demanding a doctor's prescription, but offer instant advice on health care.

The Ministry of Health has tried to reduce the price of drugs, by making it mandatory to label them with their generic name instead of their commercial name, so that people can choose the cheapest form. This attempt to offer consumer choice has been fiercely opposed by the powerful pharmaceutical industry, dominated by multinational companies, for whom the Brazilian market is extremely lucrative. It is not uncommon to see poor mothers or fathers clutching a sickly child and begging for the money to pay for the prescription they hold in their hands, which turns out to specify an expensive vitamin.

## Diagnosis: distorted priorities

Brazil's spending on health care, 7.4 per cent of the gross domestic product, would be more than enough to provide adequate services for everyone, if the resources were properly distributed. Instead, a disproportionate amount goes on hospital-based curative medicine in major cities, while preventive medicine and primary care are seriously underfunded. Government figures show that the Ministry of Health spends as much on sophisticated treatments for 12,000 patients, most of them from high-income families, as it does on treatments for 40 million people from mostly low-income families.

Eighty per cent of the people who seek treatment in the casualty departments of the public hospitals suffer from illnesses caused by contaminated water or poor sanitary conditions. One quarter of the population still has no running water, while more than one third are not connected to mains sewage systems. Considerable advances were made in the 1970s and 1980s with large, inter-nationally funded programmes for piped water and sewage systems, but spending on public health has been reduced in the last few years. As a result, diseases once considered to be under control, like tuberculosis, dengue fever, and leishmaniosis, have re-emerged. Every year there

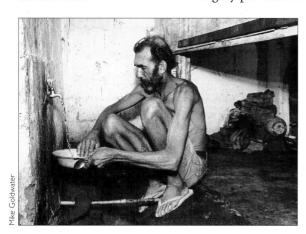

*A cane-cutter in the company shed where he lives in Petrolina. Contaminated water is a major source of disease in Brazil.*

Mike Goldwater

▲ *Malnutrition is still common, in a country that produces an abundance of food.*

are 100,000 new cases of TB. Half a million cases of malaria have been reported each year from 1990 in the Amazon region, as settlers and gold-miners move into the area and no precautions are taken to stop them catching and spreading it.

Although Brazil produces more than enough food for the needs of its population, malnutrition is still common. In the Zona da Mata area of Pernambuco, where until recently sugar-cane occupied every inch of soil, and cane-cutters were banned from planting a vegetable garden, generations of chronic malnutrition have produced populations with stunted growth. As a whole, the average height of the population of the Northeast is several inches less than in the south. In spite of widespread malnutrition, efforts to get basic foodstuffs exempted from tax have so far failed. Brazil has the highest food taxes in the world: 21 per cent on powdered milk, 34 per cent on pasta, up to 17 per cent on beans and rice. As these taxes are not charged separately, but hidden in the final price, few people realise that they are paying them.

In the 1990s the government began distributing food baskets, targetting towns with the highest infant-mortality rates (up to 180 per 1000 live births) and regions affected by the drought. This simple measure led to an immediate reduction in infant deaths, but cuts in government spending in 1999 reduced the size and number of food baskets, and rates have risen again as a consequence.

Besides the diseases of underdevelopment, Brazil also has an increasing incidence of the diseases associated with industrialisation, notably cancer and heart disease. Even when they contract the diseases of affluence, the poor are still at a disadvantage. In 1998, of the 32,695 new cases of breast cancer discovered, 80 per cent of the women had to have radical mastectomies because, without access to early diagnosis, the illness was already advanced. More than 7000 women died. Of every 100 mammography examinations, 95 are carried out in private hospitals or clinics and only five in public hospitals: an example of the very different health services available to those who can pay for them and those who cannot.

When health care is contracted out to private hospitals or organisations, the profit motive has often been put first, sometimes with fatal results. In 1997 more than 100 kidney-dialysis patients at a privately run but government-funded clinic died because of contaminated water. While Brazilian doctors are as good as anywhere in the world, performing heart transplants and pioneering surgical techniques, and the skill of the plastic surgeons is particularly well known, many public hospitals are starved of resources. In Rio women have given birth on sink tops or on the pavement because of the lack of maternity beds.

## Women's health

Women's health has never been a priority in a medical system still dominated by male doctors and influenced by the conservative morality of the Catholic Church. Pre-natal care is not available to most women, and as a result Brazil has one of the highest maternal mortality rates in the world. Millions of Brazilian women are also denied any family-planning advice. Brazil's steep drop in annual population growth, from over 6 per cent in the 1950s to 1.4 per cent in 1996, is almost entirely due to sterilisations carried out in private clinics, illegal abortions, and contraceptive pills bought over the counter at pharmacies.

In some states in the north and centre of Brazil, between one half and three quarters of all women of fertile age who do not want more children have been sterilised, many of them still in their twenties, because it is the only method of contraception available to them. More than a million clandestine abortions are believed to take place every year. Legal abortion is permitted only if rape can be proved, or the mother's life is at risk; but even in such cases, few public hospitals will perform the operation. Instead they end up treating hundreds of thousands of women who are suffering the consequences of botched back-street abortions which often leave women sterile.

## A different kind of health service

More recently there have been encouraging signs of change. The introduction of community health agents in some Brazilian states has been a big step in the right direction. The pioneer scheme was begun by the Catholic Church's Children's Pastoral, which now has a network of 100,000 neighbourhood women working as volunteer health agents, teaching child care and nutrition, linked to local churches. Several states and many municipalities have set up their own health agent schemes, linked to the Ministry of Health. The agents are chosen from local communities and trained to carry out household visits, concentrating on prevention of disease and vaccination. In most places the agents are linked to family-doctor schemes and work as part of a team, with the accent on primary health care. Brazil's major development bank BNDES (National Social and Economic Development Bank), in a welcome departure from its normal funding of Brazilian and foreign capitalist ventures, has begun to finance pioneer health schemes, like the one set up in IMIP, a maternity and children's hospital in Recife run by a charity. Called 'Mother Kangaroo', it enables the mothers of vulnerable premature babies to keep them bound to their own bodies 24 hours a day for the first crucial days or weeks – with excellent results. Because it reduces the need for incubators, the programme is highly cost-effective, and an example of how a simple but unconventional practice can often work much better than expensive technology. The Ministry of Health has decided to copy the idea and extend it to hospitals all over Brazil.

# The Northeast

## Where drought is a political issue

Brazil's Northeast is one of the poorest regions in the world. The average per capita income of the forty million people who live there is less than half the national average. This extreme poverty is traditionally blamed on the terrible droughts that periodically affect the large semi-arid zone, when it stops raining for months or years at a time. Because it is the most densely populated such zone in the world, millions of people are affected. But these droughts have never received such extensive media coverage as those in Africa, partly because the authorities have hidden their real impact. Independent sources calculated that at least 700,000 people, most of them children, died from hunger and weakness during the 1979–83 drought.

▷ *Cattle in an arid landscape, Pernambuco, Northeast Brazil*

Daniel Bernson

In 1998 another severe drought began in the semi-arid zone, lasting throughout 1999 and leaving ten million people struggling to find water. Yet the Northeast has one of Brazil's largest perennial rivers, the São Francisco, and the biggest reserves of water in the world, stored in 70,000 man-made dams and reservoirs. It has billions of cubic metres in underground water tables. The problem is distribution, not supply. The Brazilian NGOs who carried out a major survey of the 1979–83 drought concluded that it was not the drought itself that killed people, but the political use made of it by landowners and politicians as a means of increasing their power. The practice is to demand people's votes in exchange for water or jobs on the emergency work-fronts set up by the government to provide an income for the hungry. The cheap labour of hundreds of thousands of ruined small farmers has ended up favouring landowners, by being used to build roads and dams on private lands, rather than public works. Tax amnesties and special subsidies provided for drought-affected farmers rarely benefit the small subsistence farmers who make up the bulk of the population, because they often have no proper land titles.

## Caatinga: low-tech, self-help schemes for subsistence farmers

▲ João Pedro da Silva (left) discusses the drought with other farmers in Lagoa Comprida.

João Pedro da Silva is one such subsistence farmer. He lives in Lagoa Comprida near Ouricurí, in the heart of Pernambuco's semi-arid zone. To reach João Pedro's house, we drive along bumpy dirt roads between fences made of bent, gnarled branches. The trees are twisted and leafless. The dry landscape is brown; the sky is a harsh, cloudless blue. The only signs of green come from a cactus tree, the *palma*. João Pedro has lost his major crops: maize, beans, and cassava (manioc). His cattle have survived by eating the *palma* leaves that he chops up for them. The family's only income is now the old-age pension of his wife's 97-year-old father, who lives with them. But João Pedro is one of the lucky ones, because he has been able to use some of the low-cost, low-technology solutions taught by Caatinga, a Brazilian NGO. Thanks to Caatinga, the family has drinking water and has been able to save the papaya and cashew trees.

Next to the house is a Caatinga-designed underground cistern which stores rainwater and can provide a family of five with water for a year. It costs US$250. The water level is very low, but it has kept them going since the rain stopped ten months ago. To purify the now muddy water, João Pedro's wife Maria da Luz puts a few seeds from the *moringa* plant into it and leaves it to stand for a couple of hours.

In the evening we sit out in front of the house as the sun sets. The electricity promised at every election has not yet reached Lagoa Comprida. Neighbours call greetings as they go by in the dark. Everybody knows everybody in this small community. Later on, lights appear, bobbing along in the distance: a candle-lit procession of men, women, and children singing hymns makes its way to the neighbour's house. She has organised it to give thanks for her son's recovery from a broken leg. The nearest doctor is several kilometres away in the town. Eight of Maria da Luz's eleven children died, most as babies, three of them when they were teenagers disabled with what seemed to be cerebral palsy. She never discovered what was really wrong with them, or the cause of their deaths.

Next day we trudge out to João Pedro's field, a few hundred yards from the house. From the distance it looks like a little green oasis set in dry dusty fields. Closer up, we see that the banana trees are shrivelled and the leaves on the cashew trees are yellowing, but the papayas remain firm,

with bunches of large green fruits, thanks to the underground dam dug with Caatinga expertise. João Pedro and his son are digging a dam wall of loose stones, so that when the rains return and the now dried-up stream reappears, the water will be held and then filtered through the stones to make the whole area humid and fertile.

A neighbouring farmer is digging a ditch-dam, another of the ideas promoted by Caatinga. These dams are two or more metres deep and very narrow, to avoid evaporation. They capture rainwater or runoff from sloping hillsides. There is a big government dam not far away but it was badly planned and never filled enough to supply the irrigation pipes that were supposed to run from it. The only water left in the neighbourhood now is a muddy lake where people travel long distances in ox-carts to fill old oil-drums with brackish water. One of the women, Maria do Carmo da Conceição, says this is the only drinking water available for her eight children. She strains it, but does not boil it. She comes once a week with her husband in a borrowed ox-cart. Before the elections, candidates paid for lorries to travel the villages distributing water; once voting was over, they stopped. *'It's very hard for anything from the government to reach our hands. We only get something after a lot of struggle'*, says João Pedro.

Caatinga receives funding from several overseas organisations. With a staff of about 30, its aim is to work at the grassroots, finding and teaching environmentally sustainable solutions to help subsistence farmers to survive in the semi-arid area, even during times of drought. Their cisterns and small-scale dams now benefit several hundred families in the region, but could benefit thousands if the government backed such projects.

▲ *Digging a ditch-dam, designed by Caatinga staff with steep sides to avoid evaporation in the searing heat*

▼ *Francisco Alexandrino Gomes, a Caatinga worker who runs a network of seed banks to save local drought-resistant varieties of crop*

Caatinga is a member of the Permanent Committee for Dealing with the Drought, which has representatives from NGOs and the government; its staff have been invited to talk about their technology at the local HQ of the federal government's agricultural research company, Embrapa. But decisions in the region are still heavily influenced by politicians, and millions of pounds will probably be spent on a sophisticated, highly visible irrigation scheme, rather than on the low-tech but effective solutions offered by Caatinga. The staff teach local farmers how to live with the drought and find additional sources of income like animal-breeding or bee-keeping. One of them, himself a farmer, Francisco Alexandrino Gomes, runs a seed-bank network to save and develop local drought-resistant varieties. Seventy-two communities now have seed banks. *'I visit a village and ask after a certain variety. People say oh, so-and-so has it. So many seeds have disappeared over the last 20 or 30 years, and now indigenous trees like the umbuzeiro are going, because people use them for firewood.'*

Daniel Beninson

▲ *Hermes Goncalves Monteiro, Caatinga Coordinator, at the agency's headquarters*

Caatinga staff have shown farmers how to use the *palma* cactus for cattle food and how to use the seed of the *moringa*, originally an African plant, to sterilise the water. At the Caatinga centre, a series of simple low buildings surrounded by fields, coordinator Hermes Goncalves Monteiro says the origin of the region's problems is not the lack of rain, but the feudal land-ownership structure and the farming practices imported from Portugal, a country of plentiful rainfall.

## The Caatinga school

To teach the next generation how to farm sustainably, Caatinga runs a school for 200 children. The education is free, so most of the costs have to be met by the NGO, because the local authority pays only for the teachers and textbooks. These are used critically, because of their illustrations, which betray prejudiced assumptions about race and class. *'They show white middle-class models in their illustrations. Any rural workers are always shown as dirty and ragged'*, says Marli de Almeida, the school's educational adviser, herself one of the ten children of a subsistence farmer.

Through the school, Caatinga hopes to stem the rural exodus and offer teenagers an alternative to migrating to São Paulo to find work as domestic maids or labourers, which is the traditional solution for the children of poor families in the region. Some teenagers work as seasonal labourers in the newly irrigated fruit-growing areas of the São Francisco Valley, where pesticides are widely used, so teachers tell them about the dangers.

Instead of the dependency induced by decades of droughts, the children learn about solidarity and community organisation. They learn how to put into practice the alternative methods pioneered by Caatinga. They learn about the semi-arid region's medicinal plants and how to use certain leaves as food supplements. They learn to cook, to recycle paper and sell it, and to think critically about what goes on around them. According to one pupil, *'TV shows pretty things, but it doesn't show the reality of the drought. The politicians do nothing – except for the last governor, who came here and then copied the cisterns.'*

The Caatinga school has become a local reference for good education. Thirty-five teachers from rural schools in the region come here for training. The change of government every four years after elections is always a problem, because the new administrators always want to do something different. *'The authorities don't like working with NGOs, because they are ethical: they criticise corruption. The authorities don't invest in education because they want to maintain the political system as it is, with ignorant voters'*, is Marli's explanation for the lack of support.

# Babassu

Forests of what look like luxuriant green feather-dusters cover huge swathes of northern Brazil. This is the extraordinary babassu palm, a tree which supplies the raw materials for heating and lighting, shelter, food, animal feed, and even soap. The babassu thrives in the hot humid valleys of Maranhão, Piauí, Tocantins, and Pará, providing a livelihood for hundreds of thousands of families.

Breaking the small hard nuts has always been seen as women's work. Up to 300,000 *quebradeiras* (breakers) spend the day in the forest, collecting and breaking the fallen nuts. They sit on the ground, place the nut on the sharp upturned blade of a machete and break it open with blows from a stick. The kernels are then sold by the kilo. Children learn to break the babassu nut from the age of six or seven, many suffering accidents with the sharp blades. Because it is seen as women's work, boys stop doing it at around the age of 12 and go off to

▲ *Breaking babassu nuts*

work with their fathers in the fields instead, while the girls continue.

In the 1980s the babassu forests in Maranhão began to come under threat from a new type of landowner. Although the *quebradeiras* and their families, many of them descendants of freed slaves, had lived for generations on the land, it was divided up by the then state governor and handed out to political allies and companies from the south. Gunmen were brought in to expel the villagers and keep the babassu nut breakers out of the forests. Many people died in the subsequent conflicts, and almost 100,000 were evicted from their homes. Although the babassu tree is protected by a federal law that makes it illegal to cut it down, the landowners, who received government subsidies for their 'development projects', turned the land to cattle pasture or planted eucalyptus forests.

## Unity and literacy empower the *quebradeiras*

In the late 1980s, thanks to the resistance of the families who refused to give up and move to the shanty-towns in the cities, many of them were resettled on land confiscated under a government land-reform scheme.

The conflicts made people realise that only by uniting could they hope to resist the pressure from the landowners and maintain their livelihood. The *quebradeiras*, most of whom were illiterate, formed their own association, and began to write petitions to the authorities and hold meetings, first locally, then at a regional level. Instead of being ashamed of their work, they began to take pride in their identity and began to be recognised as a social force. In 1989 ASSEMA (the Association of Settlement Areas in Maranhão), a non-government organisation, began providing technical assistance to the rural communities. ASSEMA helped the *quebradeiras* to find ways of commercialising their own products, to avoid dependence on middlemen and factory owners.

Babassu soap was one result. UNICEF gave funds for a small factory to be set up in the village of Ludovico, employing 23 women. Profits are divided equally among them, and their income is twice what it would be if they simply broke the nuts. The women have learned how to do chemical analyses, but the machinery is inefficient and they lose up to 30 per cent of the soap. Some soap is sold locally, but most of it goes abroad, because in Brazil itself the concept of fair trade is not widely known or understood. Sustainable products like the babassu soap cannot compete with the well-advertised and glossily marketed commercial products available on every shop shelf. To make their soap more competitive, the women want better machines and help with marketing.

▶ *Workers in the Ludovico factory display tablets of soap made from babassu oil*

Julio Etchart

In the nearby village of Lago dos Rodrigues, another group works a press for extracting oil from the babassu nuts. The oil is then exported to the Body Shop chain in the UK, while the husks are used for animal feed. If there were more buyers, the women could expand production and benefit more families. At Esperantinopolis, a larger town in the babassu area of Maranhão, the women have set up a co-operative which buys the mesocarp, the solid pulp inside the husk, which is then powdered to make a nutritious food-supplement and sold to the local authority for mixing in school meals. But this programme is vulnerable to cuts in the school budget.

There are no government agencies to provide the expertise to improve the commercial viability of these small-scale projects, although the babassu industry provides an income for hundreds of thousands of families in one of Brazil's most impoverished areas. The government has actually reduced import taxes from 18 per cent to 2 per cent on cheap palmiste oil from abroad, so the price of babassu has slumped. Some of the larger industries that process the babassu oil have proposed mechanising the collection and breaking methods, to replace what they call the 'anachronistic practice' of the *quebradeiras*.

## ZULEIDE'S STORY

Zuleide da Silva is a *quebradeira*. She lives in Jequeri in the state of Maranhão, a village surrounded by forests of babassu. Zuleide's house has an earthen floor; a single electric bulb hangs from the centre of the rafters. The cooker stands unused, because gas is too expensive. She cooks on an earthen wood-burning stove. Shiny pots and pans hang on nails, but water has to be fetched from a neighbour's well. The bathroom is out in the yard, a small enclosure of palm fronds with a bowl. The toilet is a hole in the ground covered by a thatched shelter, up the hillside at the back of the house. Chickens scratch around everywhere, but pride of place in the yard goes to the babassu equipment. Zuleide's yard is used by half a dozen women to break the nuts they have brought in from the forest, to shell them and remove the pulp. They sit under thatch shelters to protect themselves from the hot sun.

Zuleide is a small, bustling woman who is angry that her father never let her go to school and learn to read and write. She goes to literacy classes to make up for the lost years of learning. She is very proud of her two daughters, aged 16 and 18, who are still at school. One of them wants to be a teacher. Zuleide is also proud of belonging to the local rural workers' union in her own right, not just as the wife of Luis, her husband.

In the evening a dozen women come to Zuleide's house to talk. They sit in the front room with its white-washed walls and talk about their children, their husbands, their health. They have all had lots of children – ten, eleven, twelve – and seen many of them die as babies. Seven or eight days after each birth they are back in the forest, collecting babassu nuts. The only way they know to limit their families is to 'tie the tubes', if they can find a doctor who will perform the sterilisation operation.

It is a hard life, working up to ten hours a day out of doors, come sun, come rain. The women are tired of it. Their eyesight has suffered; they have to concentrate to avoid cutting themselves with the sharp machetes: many have had accidents. They have to look out for snakes in the undergrowth and beware of rampaging cattle. And when they get home they still have to cook, do the washing, look after their children. *'There are days when I just don't want to get up'*, says Teresa, and everyone agrees. Their bodies ache. By the age of 50 they are worn out.

There is no colour bar here. One woman is black, another white, most are in between, but they share the same problems. They have tried to think of alternative ways of earning a living, like weaving baskets or making handicrafts. They cannot do embroidery, because of their bad eyesight. Their husbands work as sharecroppers, handing over a quarter or even a third of their produce to the landowners. They are allowed to plant crops, but only if they do not interfere with the grazing needs of the landowners' cattle. Many of the men travelled to the Amazon to try their luck as gold-miners; but, instead of getting rich, they came back shaking with malaria. Most of the women are illiterate, but all their children go to school. They pin all their hopes for the future on that fact.

By 9 pm everyone has gone home. In a few hours' time they must be up again, ready to make the long walk into the forest to collect the babassu nuts and begin another day of cracking them. The soap produced by the Ludovico factory carries the name *Babaçu Livre* - Free Babassu. That is the fundamental demand of the women: free access to all the babassu trees. They want the government to use its powers to confiscate all the areas where conflicts still exist, and turn the land over to settlements for the women and their families.

# The amazing Amazon

Tony Gross

## The world's largest rainforest

Boys of Paaca Nova village, fishing in the Manoré river

The sheer size of the Amazon basin region is breath-taking. Most of it lies in Brazil, but Venezuela, Colombia, Peru, Equador, and Bolivia also have regions of rainforest. The Amazon river rises in the Andes and flows for 2500 km through the forest before reaching the Atlantic Ocean. Seventeen of its tributaries are more than 600 km long. It drains an area as large as the United States, without Alaska. Marajó, the island in the mouth of the Amazon, is bigger than Denmark.

More than 200,000 indigenous people live in the Brazilian rainforest, but the Amazon basin area, which covers more than 5 million square kilometres, is no longer a sparsely populated area. Nearly 17 million Brazilians live in its towns and cities. Manaus and Belem have more than one million people each. When you fly over the green carpet of closely packed trees, it seems to stretch for ever, immense and indestructible. But already 12 per cent of this vast area has been deforested. Large-scale clearing began in the 1970s to make way for government-financed cattle ranches and colonisation projects for the settlement of small farmers displaced by dams and mechanisation in the south. Between 1978 and

1988, annual deforestation averaged 21,000 square km; since then it has slowed and then speeded up again. More recently loggers have moved in, some with government licences, many illegally.

This cycle of development began after the military who had taken power in 1964 decided to 'integrate' the region with the rest of Brazil and provide access to the rich mineral deposits revealed by aerial surveys. Work began on a network of roads, slashing through the forest from east to west and north to south, and on dozens of hydro-electric dams to provide subsidised energy for industries in other regions. The World Bank provided loans for the roads and the dams, ignoring their devastating effects on indigenous populations who happened to be in their path. To provide jobs for thousands of displaced people, a Free Trade Zone was set up in Manaus, where consumer goods were assembled under licence and sold to tourists from the wealthier south. This zone made fortunes for a small group, but surrounded Manaus with squalid shanty-towns.

## Fortunes made of rubber

The commercial exploitation of the Amazon really began a hundred years before, with the rubber boom in the late 1880s. The indigenous people had long ago discovered the water-proofing qualities of latex, but when the

▼ *Antonio da Silva Freire, tapping rubber from one of the 80 trees on his trail in the rainforest. A rubber tree, properly milked, yields latex for at least 50 years.*

Mike Goldwater

motorcar was invented and the demand for pneumatic tyres began, British and North American companies realised that they could make fortunes exporting Amazon rubber. Entire indian communities were forcibly recruited into backbreaking labour in the forest, collecting latex from rubber trees. By 1900, indian slave labour had turned Manaus into the wealthiest and most progressive city in South America, with electricity, piped water, and a tram network mostly built by the British. Famous European singers were brought to perform at the city's opera house.

Huge fortunes were made, but the boom came to an end with the advent of cheaper Malayan rubber, grown in plantations from saplings stolen from the Amazon by an Englishman, Henry Wickham, and developed at Kew Gardens. During the Second World War the Brazilian rubber industry briefly boomed again, when the Japanese occupied Malaya and the Allies turned back to the Amazon for supplies. More than 30,000 men from the impoverished Northeast were recruited; shipped direct from their native semi-arid conditions to the tropical forest, many succumbed to disease and hunger. When the war was over, the survivors were abandoned without the repatriation or the pensions they had been promised.

## Chico Mendes and the Alliance of Forest Peoples

One of the wartime rubber-tappers was the father of Chico Mendes, who was to become famous as the leader of the 20,000 rubber-tappers of Acre, before being murdered by cattle ranchers in 1988.

Mendes, who was the union president in Xapurí, organised the tappers in *empates*: collective actions when men, women, and children formed a human shield to stop the ranchers' tractors and bulldozers from clearing the forest of rubber trees to sow cattle pasture. He enlisted the help of environmentalists and went to Washington to lobby the World Bank against plans to fund a road in the region. He helped to organise the rubber-tappers' first-ever national meeting. In 1985 more than 100 tappers from 17 unions located in different areas of the Amazon travelled to the capital city, Brasilia. For many it was their first trip outside the forest. They demanded a new regional policy based on sustainable development, with the creation of special reserves, known as extractive reserves, instead of public funding for ranching and colonisation. They declared: *'We are not opposed to technology, provided that it is at our service and does not ignore our wisdom, our experience, our interests, and our rights.'*

Neil MacDonald

▲ *Chico Mendes addressing a meeting of rubber-tappers shortly before his murder in 1988*

A year later, in 1986, the rubber-collectors joined forces with their traditional enemies, the indians, to form the Alliance of Forest Peoples. *'Our fight'*, said Chico Mendes, *'is the fight of all the peoples of the forest.'* They realised that they now had a common enemy: the developers – road builders, cattle ranchers, and loggers. But these were powerful enemies. In 1988 Chico Mendes was gunned down at his own back door by ranchers. The outcry over his murder led the government to create some of the extractive reserves for which he had campaigned, one of them in Xapurí. International development agencies have provided funds to set up co-operatives, schools, and health posts in the reserves.

## Exploitation or sustainable development?

Brazilian governments, both military and civilian, have traditionally regarded the rainforest region as an asset to be exploited and 'developed', rather than a resource to be sustainably managed. Driven by more immediate interests, authorities at all levels of government have been slow to acknowledge that the Amazon has a vital contribution to make towards the future of humanity, including Brazil's own future generations.

In the early 1980s the Amazon was invaded by hundreds of thousands of gold-miners from other regions, lured by the hope of striking it rich. Entire villages in the Northeast emptied of men as they joined the gold-rush, preferring to risk their health in malarial rivers for the chance of a lucky strike, rather than toil for a pittance as rural labourers at home. Gold-mining camps became hotbeds of violence and prostitution, as bars and brothels quickly sprang up to relieve the miners of any cash they had earned. Many died in mud-slides, in diving accidents, or drunken brawls. Others died from malaria. Known only by their nicknames, many of them were buried anonymously in unmarked graves. From the government's point of view, the gold-rush served to take the pressure off demands for land reform.

The latest threat to the Amazon region now comes from agriculture. With government encouragement, the soya plantations of central Brazil are spreading north into the basin area. New export corridors are being created to carry the grain. Rivers like the Madeira and the Tocantins-Araguaia complex are being turned into industrial waterways for grain barges. Small Amazon ports are being turned into container terminals and timber depots. Roads are being paved to carry heavy traffic.

Satellite images from Brazil's space-research centre, INPE, have helped to create awareness of the alarming rate of deforestation in the Amazon. In one year alone, the ten worst deforesters destroyed and burned the equivalent of 32,700 soccer pitches to plant cattle grass. Left intact, the rainforest acts as a 'carbon sink', absorbing carbon dioxide from the atmosphere; but huge forest fires, some of them covering hundreds of square kilometres, throw vast quantities of greenhouse gases into the air.

Brazilian environmentalists who defend the preservation of the Amazon find themselves the target of absurd accusations: they are allegedly 'threatening the sovereignty of Brazil', by playing into the hands of multinational mining corporations, who do not want competition from the minerals of the Amazon. Yet international pressure has been vital. In 1989 the Brazilian government set up an environment agency to protect not only the rainforest but all conservation areas and threatened species. With a limited budget and small staff, this agency, IBAMA, has been

▼ *Rainforest timber feeds the kilns that produce the charcoal that is needed in vast quantities for the processing of iron ore*

Jenny Matthews

▲ *An Ashaninka man hunting with bow and arrow in the rainforest near the border with Peru*

unable to cover Brazil's vast area. (It is worth remembering that all of Europe can easily fit into the Amazon region.) In 1992 the World Bank and the G7 group of the world's richest industrialised countries drew up with Brazil a US$250 million dollar Pilot Programme to Conserve the Brazilian Rainforest. The aim of the Programme is to reduce deforestation by encouraging sustainable development projects for both natural and human resources. The German government donated a specific amount for the demarcation of indigenous reserves. Non-government organisations were intended to play an important part in setting up and running projects, and a special sub-programme was created to fund them. In the same year, 1992, more than 400 Amazon NGOs set up a network called the GTA (Amazon Work Group) to administer government funds for indigenous and non-indigenous organisations, like the extractive reserves for rubber-tappers. The GTA also provides feedback for the Pilot Programme funders.

The Amazon rainforest is a treasure chest of biodiversity. Each acre can contain nearly 200 tree species. It teems with insect life, with birds, amphibians, primates, and plant species, many of them unique to the area, many of them unstudied. Often by subterfuge, pharmaceutical companies have already carried off many plant species known to the indigenous populations for their medicinal properties and patented their active principles for commercial drugs. Although these drugs then bring huge profits for the companies, the indigenous communities receive no recognition for the centuries of knowledge that have gone into discovering the medicinal use of certain plants; nor do they benefit in the form of royalties.

▶ *Spirits of the forest lament its destruction: a painting by Brazilian artist Helio Melo*

# Football

For people everywhere Brazil means, above all, football. The only country to win the World Cup four times, Brazil has produced generations of talented players, among them Pelé (real name Edson Arantes do Nascimento), probably the most famous soccer player of all time. Dancing to the hip-shaking music of samba and *frevo* from childhood, Brazilians seem to have a natural advantage when it comes to dribbling and controlling the ball.

Daniel Berinson

It is hard to believe that at first soccer was considered to be a white man's sport, played in exclusive clubs from which blacks were banned. The game arrived in Brazil from England in 1884 and spread rapidly in clubs and on the streets. In 1921, when a team was being selected to take part in the South American Championship in Argentina, the Brazilian president ordered an all-white team to be chosen, to avoid the 'shame' of being represented by black players. Thus deprived of some of the best players, Brazil lost. The clubs wanted to recruit black players, not because they were anti-racist, but because they needed their skills. New rules were introduced by the Football Federation in an attempt to stop them. For example, knowing that many of the black players were illiterate, a new rule prescribed that each player must sign his name before a match. The clubs got round this by hiring teachers, to teach illiterate players not how to read and write, but simply how to write their signatures. When they played, black players were expected to be deferential to the white players; if they committed an offence on the field, the penalties were greater. It was only when black players like Pele and Garrincha ensured Brazilian victories in the World Cup championships of 1958 and 1962 that they were fully accepted, and their graceful, creative football came to be regarded as the best in the world. Today the Brazil team fields players of every colour.

## The politicisation of football

In 1970, after Brazil had won the World Cup for the third time, the military regime recognised the political advantage to be gained by encouraging the national passion; they hoped it would divert people's attention from their wretched economic and social conditions. Huge stadia were built in almost every state capital. The national league was widened to include clubs from every corner of Brazil, of every standard and quality. Football became mixed with politics. Candidates sought votes by donating uniforms to local clubs; politicians got themselves elected as club chairmen; footballers ran for election as city councillors or state deputies – although, once elected, they usually proved to be ineffectual as politicians. Top-league clubs were heavily subsidised by national lottery money, and exempt from income tax. They made fortunes for some of the *cartolas*, the bosses – invariably pro-government politicians – who ran them.

With the return to civilian government, football exchanged its political allegiances for commercial sponsorship. Lucrative contracts turned some players into millionaires, and the Brazil team was accused of deciding its fixtures according to the interests of its major sponsor. Even so, football continues to inspire a passion that nothing else can match. During World Cup matches, green and yellow, the national colours, appear everywhere. As the hour of the match draws nearer, the streets empty; most shops, factories, and offices close down as the entire nation gathers round its television sets or radios. For poor boys, to be signed by a professional team remains one of the few routes out of poverty. Ronaldo, now the world's wealthiest player, began life in a working suburb of Rio. Romário, whose rebellious nature has never allowed him to become a world star, grew up in a shanty-town.

Frances Rubin

▲ *Even priests play football: Belém street mural during the 1982 World Cup*

# Carnival

### The biggest song and dance spectacle on earth

Few things are taken more seriously in Brazil than Carnival. The entire country comes to a standstill for four and a half days, ending at mid-day on Ash Wednesday, the first day of the Christian season of Lent. For those taking part in the giant parades of the *escolas de samba*, literally the samba schools, in Rio de Janeiro or São Paulo, it is the culmination of months of work and rehearsals. Teams of helpers have been sewing costumes and preparing the elaborate floats. There is even a profession – *carnavalesco* – the person who organises the entire performance, which can involve up to three thousand dancers and drummers. The big schools are still based in shanty-towns, but nowadays celebrities – TV actors, models, footballers, and professional singers – are also invited to take part. Middle-class Brazilians and tourists can pay to dance in the parade, although they are hidden away where their lack of rhythm will not be conspicuous. The dancers, musicians, and floats are closely scrutinised by a panel of experts, who award points for harmony, percussion, punctuality, and costumes. The choice of winner, and the protests of the losers, are headline news. Government ministers, sometimes the President himself, business tycoons, playboys, famous footballers, personalities of all sorts watch the Rio Carnival from luxurious boxes sponsored by local authorities and private companies, where food and drink flow freely. Behind the scenes, the organised crime gangs who run the illegal gambling game known as the *jogo do bicho* provide funding for some of the schools.

But the Carnival parade is not just an exuberant explosion of noise and colour. It has traditionally been used as an occasion for social and political criticism. Well-known social militants like Betinho (Herbert de Souza), who in 1993 launched a nationwide campaign against hunger involving 4000 local committees, have taken part. Once a contingent from SWAPO, the

▼ *Dancing in the streets: Brazilians have a natural sense of rhythm*

Julio Etchart

Namibian freedom movement, marched in a samba school. Members of the MST, the Landless Rural Workers' Movement, have paraded. Sometimes the choice of theme becomes a national issue. A few years ago the Archbishop of Rio went to court to stop one school using a giant replica of the Christ statue that overlooks the city from Corcovado mountain as part of their Carnival theme about the homeless. Undaunted, the samba school wrapped their statue in black plastic so that it could not be seen; but everyone knew what it was, and the parade went ahead. In 1988 another school chose the satirical magazine *O Pasquim*, heavily censored by the military, as its theme and had floats portraying giant instruments of torture and a group of dwarfs dressed as generals.

While street parades and balls are the highlight of the Carnival in Rio and São Paulo, celebrations take different forms in other major Brazilian cities. Olinda, the historic town next to Recife, claims the biggest street carnival, with up to two million people dancing all through the night and into the day, behind giant puppet figures to the frenetic *frevo* rhythm. In Salvador, the Bahian capital, the crowds dance behind 200 *trios eletricos* – large trucks carrying bands and singers. Bahia, the state with the largest black population in Brazil, demonstrates a remarkable degree of musical creativity, with Afro-Brazilian groups introducing new rhythms every year, mixing religious music from *candomblé* ceremonies with reggae, samba, and jazz. The Afro groups have powerful drum bands which play a beat reminiscent of war drums, and invent their own dance steps. All-female groups have appeared, and for them carnival is a festival of emancipation. In small old towns in Minas Gerais and Goiás, the pre-Lenten celebrations have a more religious tone, with mock battles between Christians and pagans on horseback.

Carnival lasts less than a week, but the social, cultural, and sports activities developed by some of the big samba schools like Mangueira in Rio and the drum group Olodum in Salvador continue throughout the year. Working with some of the poorest children in the community, Olodum teaches children to respect themselves and demand respect, and provides them with a sense of identity, a sense of belonging.

# Conclusion

Travelling around Brazil to do the research for this book, I visited cities, towns, and rural zones in the North and Northeast where most Oxfam-funded projects are located. On the banks of an Amazon river, in the scorching heat of the semi-arid zone, in the mud-and-wattle huts of an occupation community, in the forests of babassu palms, I met scores of men and women, black, white, and indian, who are planning, working, and organising to create a fairer, less unequal, society.

They know what they want: a society where decent housing, education, health care, and transport services are not the privilege of the few, but the right of the many. Where public policies are designed to serve the majority, not the influential minority. Where children go to school, not to work cutting cane, scouring waste-tips for food, or stoking charcoal ovens. Where the forests and rivers are respected and valued for their biodiversity, not devastated and contaminated in the search for profit. And where they have as much right to decide what their country's priorities should be as the bankers and technocrats do.

These men and women, and hundreds of thousands of others like them all over Brazil, have grown tired of hearing unfulfilled promises of a better future that never arrives. They have decided to make it happen.

*Jan Rocha*

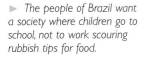
▶ *The people of Brazil want a society where children go to school, not to work scouring rubbish tips for food.*

Daniel Beninson

# Facts and figures

**Land area:**
8.5 million square km
(47 per cent of South America)

**Population:**
163 million (1999)

**Population growth rate:**
1.4 per cent p.a. (1996)

**Urban population:**
78 per cent (1996)

**Average life expectancy:**
men 63 years, women: 71 years

**Households without piped water:**
24 per cent

**Households without mains sewerage:**
30 per cent

**Adult literacy:**
83 per cent

**Infant mortality:**
36 deaths per 1000 live births
(59 in Northeast)

**Number of children under 18 in poverty:**
21 million (living in families with per capita
income of less than half the national
minimum wage)

**Number of children of primary-school age
(7–14) not in school:**
1.3 million

**Number of children aged 5–14 working:**
2.9 million; aged 10–14: 5.7 million

**Proportion of deaths of young people in São
Paulo aged 15–24 caused by violence:**
67 per cent (road accidents, murder, suicide)

**Gross domestic product:**
US$ 775 billion (1998)

**Income per capita:**
US$4,790 (1998)

**Foreign debt:**
US$200 billion (1998)

**Economic growth:**
0.1 per cent (1998)

**Principal exports:**
manufactures, iron ore, soybeans, coffee,
meat, sugar

**Main trading partners:**
USA, EU, Argentina

**Currency:**
the Real; average exchange rate:
R$1.83 = US$1.00 (1999)

(Sources: Economist Intelligence Unit: *Brazil:
Country Profile 1999-2000* and *Brazil: Country
Report, Last Quarter, 1999*; UNICEF: *The State
of the World's Children, 1999.*)

Andrew Couldridge

# Dates and events

**10,000 BC**  First known presence of human beings in the Americas.

**3000 BC**  Probable beginning of *tupi-guarani*, one of the main Brazilian indian language systems

**22 April 1500**  Portuguese explorer Pedro Alvares Cabral, looking for passage to the spice islands of the East, lands on coast of Bahia, names it Vera Cruz and claims it for the Portuguese crown

**1549**  Colonial rule established in Bahia

**1695**  Gold discovered in Minas Gerais

**1768**  Capital moved from Salvador to Rio de Janeiro

**1792**  Tiradentes, leader of failed uprising against Portuguese, executed

**1808**  Portuguese royal family flees to Brazil to escape Napoleon

**1822**  Independence declared by Pedro, Crown Prince of Portugal, who becomes Emperor of Brazil

**1850**  Slave traffic stopped

**1888**  Slavery abolished

**1889**  Monarchy abolished. Brazil becomes a republic

**1930**  Getúlio Vargas takes power after military coup; dictatorship lasts until 1945

**1955**  Juscelino Kubitschek elected; launches programme of industrialisation, and construction of Brasilia

**1960**  Capital moved from Rio de Janeiro to Brasilia

**1964**  Military coup and beginning of 21-year dictatorship

**1980**  Workers' Party (PT) founded

**1984**  Landless Rural Workers' Movement (MST) founded

**1985**  Return to civilian rule: President Tancredo Neves dies before taking office, succeeded by Vice-president José Sarney

**1988**  Chico Mendes shot dead

**1989**  PT presidential candidate Lula loses to Fernando Collor

**1992**  Collor resigns to avoid impeachment for corruption

**1993**  Annual inflation exceeds 2000 per cent

**1994**  Real Plan launched; Fernando Henrique Cardoso elected President

**1998**  Cardoso re-elected

**1999**  Brazil devalues currency: economic crisis

# Sources and further reading

Amnesty International: *Beyond Despair: Amnesty International Report on Human Rights in Brazil*, London: Amnesty International, 1994

Medea Benjamin and Maisa Mendonca: *Benedita da Silva* (the story of Brazil's first black woman senator), London: Latin America Bureau, 1998

*Beyond All Pity: The Diary of Carolina Maria de Jesus*, London: Earthscan, 1990

Sue Branford and Oriel Glock: *The Last Frontier: Fighting over Land in the Amazon*, London: Zed Books, 1985

Sue Branford and Bernardo Kucinski: *Brazil: Carnival of the Oppressed – Lula and the Workers' Party*, London, Latin America Bureau, 1995

Gilberto Dimenstein: *Brazil: War on Children*, London: Latin America Bureau, 1991

*Fala Favela*, photographs and booklet, Dublin and Birmingham: Trocaire and the Development Education Centre, 1991 (for 11–18 year olds)

Gilberto Freyre: *The Mansions and the Shanties: the making of modern Brazil*, University of California, 1986

Duncan Green: *Silent Revolution, the rise of market economics in Latin America*, London: Cassell, 1995

Susanna Hecht and Alexander Cockburn: *The Fate of the Forests: Developers, Destroyers and Defenders of the Amazon*, New York: Harper, 1990

Robert Levine and John J. Crocitti (eds): *The Brazil Reader*, London: Latin America Bureau, 1999

Gordon MacMillan: *At the End of the Rainbow? Gold, Land and People in the Brazilian Amazon*, London: Earthscan, 1995

Stephen McCarthy: *In Search of Eldorado*, Dublin: Trocaire, 1996 (for 12–18 year olds)

Chico Mendes and Tony Gross: *Fight for the Forest: Chico Mendes in his own words*, London: Latin America Bureau, 1992

Fr Ricardo Rezende: *Rio Maria: Song of the Earth*, London and Dublin: CIIR and Trocaire, 1994

Jan Rocha: *Brazil in Focus*, London: Latin America Bureau, 1997

Jan Rocha: *Murder in the Rainforest: the Yanomami, the Goldminers and the Amazon*, London: Latin America Bureau, 1999

Thomas Skidmore: *Brazil: Five Centuries of Change*, Oxford: Oxford University Press, 1999

Thomas Skidmore and Peter Smith: *Modern Latin America*, Oxford: Oxford University Press, 1992

Alison Sutton: *Slavery in Brazil*, London: Anti-Slavery Society, 1995

*Views from Brazil: Introducing Development Issues*, Dublin and Birmingham: Trocaire and the Development Education Centre, 1990

*Women in Brazil*, London: Latin America Bureau for Caipora Women's Group, 1993

## Sources

Commissão Pastoral da Terra, *Trabalho Escravo no Brasil Contemporâneo,* Edicoes Loyola 1999

Bernardo Kucinski: *O Síndrome da Antena Parabolica: Etica No Jornalismo Brasileiro,* Editora Fundação Perseu Abramo, São Paulo 1998

Bernardo Mançano Fernandes: *Gênese e Desenvolvimento do MST,* Editora Peres, 1998

UNICEF: *The State of the World's Children,* Oxford: Oxford University Press, 1999

Alfredo Wagner: *As quebradeiras de côco de babaçu*

Daniel Berinson

◀ *Boys in Recife practising capoeira, a martial-art dance-form popular with street children*

# Acknowledgements

My thanks are due to photographer Daniel Berinson, for being an excellent travelling companion, considerate and cheerful. ... To the families with whom we stayed while researching the book – Maria da Luz and João Pedro in Lagoa Comprida, Zuleide and her daughters in Esperantinópolis, Francisco and Celia and their family in the Apuriná village at Boca do Acre – for allowing us to share their homes, their meals, and their lives for a few days. ... To the members of Oxfam's partner organisations who organised our trip and found time to accompany us and inform us, especially Lucineide and Salles at FAMCC, and Luciene and Maria Alaide at ASSEMA. ... To Claude St-Pierre and the staff at the Recife Oxfam office, especially Jessica Pelham, for their painstaking correction of the first draft. ... And last but not least to editor Catherine Robinson, for her patience and understanding throughout.

*Jan Rocha*

▼ *Work can be fun: children of the Pedra Vermelha settlement, Northeast Brazil*

Daniel Berinson

# Oxfam in Brazil

Levels of inequality between rich and poor are higher in Brazil than almost anywhere else in the world, and Brazil is the largest country in the world with an Oxfam programme of social development. Oxfam works in the poorest regions: the Amazon and the Northeast, which are comparable with some of the poorest countries in the world in terms of their income per capita, and the quality of their health and education services. Most of the people and projects featured in this book have received support from Oxfam, and the stories illustrate how poverty affects a wide range of social groups.

Since 1968, Oxfam has been working with the most vulnerable groups in Brazilian society, including indigenous peoples, descendants of runaway slaves, the urban poor (including black communities, women, and street children), the landless and the rural poor. Oxfam has a wide range of partners, including grassroots organisations, community groups, trade unions, and local and national non-government organisations and networks. Most of Oxfam's work is geared towards long-term sustainable development, but it also undertakes emergency relief work in times of severe drought or flooding.

In the Amazon, Oxfam helps indigenous peoples to campaign for the demarcation of their traditional lands, thereby securing legal tenure to them. Oxfam also defends indigenous peoples' cultural rights and languages. In addition, several Oxfam partners deliver essential health services to indigenous groups. Other beneficiaries in this region include communities who collect brazil and babassu nuts, who are helped in their efforts to reach new markets and to defend their rights to access the forest.

In the semi-arid zone of Northeast Brazil, Oxfam helps small-scale farmers and indigenous groups to make a living in what is a harsh and drought-prone region. Ensuring access to a safe water supply is the top priority, but secondary activities include developing goat rearing, planting drought-resistant crops, and campaigning for land tenure. Oxfam helps to influence local and national policies, and works in partnership with international charities and other funders, maximising efforts to reduce abject poverty in the region.

Urban poverty is increasing in both the Amazon and the Northeast. Oxfam supports a series of initiatives, including lobbying local municipalities to provide urban services such as basic sanitation, clean water, sewage treatment, and rubbish collection. Oxfam also supports communities in shanty-towns, helping them to secure land tenure and decent housing.

Brazil's democracy is young and fragile, and most of its voters are ignorant of their rights, unaware that a generous but largely overlooked constitution already exists to protect them. Oxfam believes it is vital to voice the needs of the forgotten poor, helping them to assert their right to a say in their futures. Oxfam is helping local organisations to develop their in-country fundraising skills, reducing their dependency on international sources of funding. Oxfam's partners are developing their supporter bases, which in turn will improve their lobby work, helping them to raise awareness among Brazilians of the country's critical social problems and practical solutions to them. Local organisations receive training in campaigning methods and communications, and Oxfam provides financial support for fundraising activities.

Because Oxfam believes that it is not possible to reduce poverty by working alone, it continues to forge and strengthen partnerships in Brazil. It also lobbies international financial institutions to adopt and implement policies that will benefit impoverished people.

▼ 'Together we are strong': a Macuxi community in Cantagalo village, Roraima

Daniel Bennson

# Index

land theft 6, 9–12, 22, 30, 37–8, 67
liberation theology 34, 43
literacy 27, 41, 52, 56, 58, 69
logging 11, 15, 71
Ludovico 68, 69
Lula 42–3, 44–5, 45, 53

Macuxi 57, 86
Madeira river 14, 73
malnutrition 10–11, 61
Manaus 70, 71
Maranhão 67, 68, 69
Mato Grosso do Sul 58
MDB 42
media ownership 52–3
medicines
    traditional 12, 66, 74
Mendes, Chico 72
migration 21, 31
military regime 33–6, 47–8, 52
mining: *see* gold; iron-ore
moringa seeds 66
MPA 25
MST 21–5, 40, 57, 77–8
Mura 57

Nambiquara 10
newspapers 54
NGOs 54, 58, 63, 66, 68, 74

Olinda 78
Oxfam 79, 85, 86

palma cactus 66
Palmares 17
Pantanal 5
Paraguai river 5
Parakaná 10
Paraná river 5
PDT 42, 55
Peasant Leagues 20
Pelé 18, 75
Pernambuco 24, 61
PFL 45
pharmaceuticals 74
Pilot Programme to Conserve the
    Brazilian Rainforest 12, 74
Pinheiro, Paula Sergio 38
PMDB 45
police 20, 23–4, 32, 37–9
POLIS 32
political parties 41, 42
politics 7, 33–6, 41, 53–
Porto Alegre 32

poverty 6–7, 51, 63, 80, 85
Prezeis programme 32
privatisation, state industry 51
prostitution 59, 73
protests 33, 35–6, 41
PSDB 45
PT: *see* Workers' Party
PTB 42
public policy 79

*quebradeiras* 67–9
*quilombos* 17, 19

race 16–19, 38, 41, 75–6
radio 13, 54
rainforest 12, 70, 72–3, 74
Real Plan 49–50
Recife 30, 32, 33
religion 6, 21, 34, 43, 78
    *see also* Catholic Church
resettlements 67–8
Rio de Janeiro 17, 30
Rio Grande do Sul 32, 57
road-building 9, 35, 71
rubber 71–2

Salvador 78
São Francisco river 5, 63
São Francisco Valley 66
São Paulo 19, 30, 31, 37
Sarney, José 54
school meals 50, 56, 59
schools 26–7, 55
    *see also* education
seed banks 65
self-help projects 23–4
shamans 15
da Silva, Benedita 19
da Silva, Zuleide 69
slavery 16–17, 71
small farmers 10, 20, 24, 25, 63–6
soap-making 68
social service 31, 50
soya 10, 73
street children 37, 59, 83
SUDENE 50
sugar 12, 46, 58
Suruí 10, 11
sustainable development 72–3, 85

Tocantins-Araguaia river complex 73
trade unions 47
transport 31
TV Globo 19, 36, 53

UDR 21
UN Human Development Index 7
unemployment 25, 48
Uni-Acre 13
UNICEF 59, 68, 80
universities 19, 55–6
urban population 26–32, 80, 85

Vargas, Getúlio 47
Vargas, Yvette 42
Viana, Jorge 13
Vila Irmã Dulce 26, 28–9
Vila Padre Cícero 29, 30
violence 38–9, 73
    *see also* police
voting 19, 41, 63–4

wages 17, 58, 80
Waimiri Atroari 10
waste recycling 7, 59
water resources 5, 63
water supplies 26, 28, 60, 63–6, 80
women
    activism 15, 19
    Carnival 78
    health care 62
    reproductive rights 43
    sexual exploitation 17
    violence against 39
Workers' Party 13, 32, 42–3, 59
World Bank 22, 72

Xavante 11
Xucuru 57

Yanomami 6, 10, 11, 38, 57

Zumbí 17, 19